GREENBERG'S GUIDE TO
LGB TRAINS

By John R. Ottley

Edited by Carter Colwell
With the assistance of
Linda F. Greenberg and **Donna W. Price**

Photographic plates supplied courtesy of
Lehmann-Gross-Bahn, Nurnburg

```
DEDICATION


To Dad
```

Copyright 1986

Greenberg Publishing Company
7543 Main Street
Sykesville, MD 21784
(301) 795-7447

First Edition

Manufactured in the United States of America

Greenberg Publishing Company offers the world's largest selection of Lionel, American Flyer and other toy train publications as well as a selection of books on model and prototype railroading. To receive our current catalogue, send a stamped, self-addressed envelope marked "Catalogue."

Greenberg Publishing Company sponsors the world's largest public model train shows. The shows feature extravagant operating model railroads for N, H0, 0, Standard and 1 gauges as well as a huge marketplace for buying and selling nearly all model railroad equipment. The shows feature, as well, a large selection of dollhouse miniatures.

Shows are currently offered in Philadelphia, Pittsburgh, Baltimore, Boston, Norfolk, Fort Lauderdale and Tampa. To receive our current show listing, please send a stamped, self-addressed envelope marked "Train Show Schedule."

Library of Congress Cataloging-in-Publication Data

Ottley, John R.
    Greenberg's guide to LGB trains.

    Includes index.
    1. Railroads—Models. 2. Ernst Paul Lehmann (Firm)
I. Colwell, C. Carter. II. Title.
TF197.077 1986   625.1'9   86-18311
ISBN 0-89778002-7

Table of Contents

Acknowledgments

A great number of collectors, operators, dealers and enthusiasts contributed to this book.

John Ottley provided the inspiration and basic manuscript. His detailed and accurate listings plus his tremendous willingness to tell the story well made working with him an enjoyable and constructive experience. **Carter Colwell**, editor, was a real find. His insistence on clarity and his writing and editing skills substantially increased the breadth of the final publication. **Donna Price**, staff copy editor and graphic artist, organized the original materials and interspersed prototypical information from the catalogues with toy train text. She also executed the line drawings, designed the book's layout and positioned the text.

Throughout, **Wolfgang Richter** encouraged our endeavor and assisted us in obtaining information and photographs from the LGB catalogue archives. Those photographs, without names of specific collectors, are all from the LGB archives. His hospitality when Carter Colwell visited him in Nuremberg, and his subsequent informal but informative visits with John Ottley in California, helped tremendously in the accurate and complete collection of data. As a model of business acumen and exuberant vitality, Wolfgang Richter is a mentor par excellence.

Jack Barton, Bob Cage, Decker Doggett, Rudi Enners and **Don Herzog**, all long-standing LGB operators and collectors, and **Joe Hylva**, who, in addition to being a well-known collector is also a very active LGB seller, all assisted by comparing their trains and knowledge with the text and made many very helpful corrections and additions. **Robert Rench** and **Vernon Winn** met with Bruce and me and carefully reviewed equipment and slides of the LGB factory. **Al Rudman** of **Trackside Hobbies** generously lent many trains from his collection to be photographed, including the 2018D shown on the cover. Al, a very busy but very gracious man, spent considerable time with us in reviewing LGB sets and unusual items. **George Ryall** and **Mike Twiford** also lent trains and equipment to be photographed. Most of the new color plates were taken by **Earl Sakowski** of **Mettee Photography**; others were taken by Carter Colwell; while the black and white photographs were taken by Bruce Greenberg and printed by **George Stern** and **Tim Parrish.**

In addition, I very much appreciate the eagerness, diligence and care taken by the number of readers who helped read and check (and double-check) the manuscript. Their knowledge and willingness to assist significantly improved the book's usefulness. Readers included: **Peter Altonna, Jack Barton, Bob Cage, Decker Doggett, Bill Gallagher, John Henderson, Jan Heine, Don Herzog, Joe Hylva, Bill Johnson, Ed Meister, George Nicholson, Len Ottley, Frank Pac, Robert Rench, Marie Richter, Clinton Ross, Al Rudman,** of **Trackside Hobbies, George Ryall, Bob Schuster, Charles Shaffer, Mike Twiford, Dave Weiler** and **Vernon Winn.**

Finally, **Barbara Brown** integrated Carter's final editing and helped shepherd the manuscript from the various reviewers to final production.

The authors invite collectors to participate in the collection of additional data regarding LGB trains. If you have a variation which is not listed in this book, or a question regarding the details of an item described herein, please use the enclosed Addition/Correction sheet to update our records. If you have a specific question, please write to John Ottley at the Greenberg Publishing Company. We welcome all comments and suggestions.

Linda Greenberg
Publisher

Foreword

PURPOSE

The purpose of this book is to provide a history and comprehensive listing with current values for Lehmann-Gross-Bahn (**LGB**) equipment and trains. We include those variations which have been authenticated. In a few cases, where data is missing or doubtful we ask readers for further information or confirmation. Values are reported for items which are not available from current dealer stock.

DETERMINING VALUES

Toy train values vary for a number of reasons. First, consider the **relative knowledge** of the buyer and seller. A seller may be unaware that he has a rare variation and sell it for the price of a common piece. Another source of price variation is **short-term fluctuation**. If four 2040s are for sale at a small meet, we would expect that supply would quickly outpace demand and lead to a reduction in price. A related source of variation is the **season** of the year. The train market is slower in the summer, and sellers may at this time be more inclined to reduce prices if they really want to move an item. Another important source of price variation is the relative strength of the seller's **desire to sell** and the buyer's **eagerness to buy**. Clearly a seller in economic distress will be more eager to strike a bargain. A final source of variation is the **personalities** of the seller and buyer. Some sellers like to turn over items quickly and, therefore, price their items to move; others seek a higher price and will bring an item to meet after meet until they find a willing buyer.

CONDITION FOR VALUE

EXCELLENT: Item has unblemished factory paint and details, may or may not have box, has signs of light indoor running (i.e. pickup shoes show some wear but are not overly worn and the wheels have minor scuffing). In contrast, MINT means that the item is brand new, absolutely unmarred, is completely original and unused, and is in its original box. GOOD means that the item has blemished paint, has signs of heavy indoor running (i.e., the pickup shoes show considerable wear and the wheels show heavy scuffing). Thus, MINT brings a higher price than EXCELLENT, and EXCELLENT brings a higher price than GOOD.

Among most toy train collectors there is a great deal of concern with exterior appearance and less concern with operation. The exception to this rule is LGB enthusiasts. LGB enthusiasts are generally as impressed with the train's running ability as with its outward appearance. Therefore, if operation is important to you, you must ask the seller whether the train runs. If the seller indicates that he does not know whether the equipment operates, you should test it. Most train meets have test tracks provided for that purpose.

We receive many inquiries as to whether or not a particular piece is a "good value." This book will help answer that question; but, there is NO substitute for experience in the marketplace. WE STRONGLY RECOMMEND THAT NOVICES DO NOT MAKE MAJOR PURCHASES WITHOUT THE ASSISTANCE OF FRIENDS WHO HAVE EXPERIENCE IN BUYING AND SELLING TRAINS. If you are buying a train and do not know whom to ask about its value, look for the people running the meet or show and discuss with them your need for assistance. Usually they can refer you to an experienced collector who will be willing to examine the piece and offer his opinion.

PRICING CODE

CP — CURRENT PRODUCTION. The item is readily available for purchase from current dealer stocks. The price fluctuates somewhat according to exchange rate, the seller's cost basis and local competition.

NRS — NO REPORTED SALES. In the few cases where there is insufficient information upon which to determine the value of a given item, we show **NRS** in the price column. Here again we recommend that you rely on your **experience** or on the **assistance** of an experienced collector to determine what price you should pay for any of these items.

NSS — NOT SOLD SEPARATELY. Originally sold as part of a set and not intended for individual sale, however some dealers and/or collectors may have broken sets up.

If you have trains to sell and you sell them to a person planning to resell them, you will not obtain the prices reported in this book. Rather, you should expect to achieve about seventy-five percent of these prices. Basically, for your items to be of interest to a buyer who plans to resell them, he must purchase them for considerably less than the prices listed here.

NUREMBERG AND NURNBERG

There are two spellings of the name Nuremberg which appear in the book. The German spelling "Nurnberg" is used when it refers to specific markings on trains and should be taken as having an umlaut (two dots) over the letter u. The American spelling "Nuremberg" is used at all other times.

Letters in parentheses are not part of LGB's car numbering system but have been added by the author to help differentiate between model variations.

Introduction

By John Ottley

Although only seventeen years have elapsed since Lehmann first began producing trains, numerous changes and continual upgrading have improved the quality of LGB trains while generating many interesting and unusual variations. With LGB's accelerating popularity has also come a greater desire by collectors to understand and decipher the nature and value of this new collectible. These circumstances, coupled with the opportunity to capture all of LGB's rare or little known variations while the product is still new, make this collector's guide both unique and valuable.

However, the information provided here is not just for the "serious" collector; it is also intended to be used on a casual basis to help the sporadic operator discover more about his enjoyable toy and how it happens to be a wise investment in many ways.

LGB, K, G AND IIm:
A WORD ON SCALE AND GAUGE

When LGB (Lehmann-Gross-Bahn) trains first began rolling off the assembly lines at the Lehmann factory in Nuremberg, West Germany in 1968, most toy manufacturers considered the 1:22.5 scale toy train too large and awkward to be a practical toy. As we have seen, these early doomsayers were wrong. LGB trains, whose robust qualities allow them to be run either indoors or outside, have experienced an expanding popularity of historic proportion. Not only has LGB been successful, but it has played a major role in rekindling public interest in toy trains.

The trains themselves are modeled primarily on European and American narrow gauge prototypes in 1:22.5 scale currently known as G Gauge. The G designation was an imaginative designation utilized to better promote the line and to distinguish it from other large scale trains. In this country, LGB was originally designated by the first U. S. Distributor, Chas. C. Merzbach Co., as K Gauge to emphasize its king size. However, in the mid-1970s the designation was changed to G to bridge more appropriately the German (gross) and English (giant) language barrier.

These size designations, with the fact that LGB runs on track with the same distance between the rails as 1 Gauge (45 mm), have caused considerable confusion among collectors and modelers as to just what gauge LGB really is. To Europeans, 1:22.5 translates into Scale II (2). LGB, which is 1:22.5 scale running on 45 mm gauge track (Scale II trains on Gauge I track), is for them IIm Scale (scale II, meter-width narrow gauge.) In the United States, many collectors still refer to LGB as 1 Gauge, while free thinkers have gone so far as to give it a "Gm" Gauge. Despite LGB's popularity, the G designation has not been universally embraced. Indeed, nearly all European manufacturers of 1:22.5 scale trains designate their products as gauge II. In the name of universal understanding and accuracy, LGB should be called gauge IIm as well, with G as a synonym. If and when the G designation receives wider acceptance, the "Gm" application may become appropriate. At present, GM is known to our European friends only as an American manufacturer of automobiles!

Wolfgang Richter and John Ottley

SOME PERSONAL HISTORY

My first active involvement with LGB happened only four years ago. Although some people may not see any correlation between the change I went through because of my experience with LGB trains, I am sure that Sigmund Freud would find an interesting connection in the story that follows.

In mid-1982, while finishing up the live animal research for my Master's Degree in Herpetology (reptile and amphibian studies), I began looking for a hobby that didn't need to be fed or have its cage cleaned. As I mulled over possible alternatives, I began to remember with very pleasant and positive associations the toy trains I had played with as a child. The seeds planted by Marx windup choo-choos, nurtured by American Flyer and Lionel, suddenly began to sprout! I remembered early train layouts covering sheets of plywood, and rails and trains running all through the house.

These thoughts and memories evoked an idyllic vision of track running from room to room through my home, and of my happiness as I lie on the front room carpet with my children as we all watch the trains whiz by. But, perhaps the best part of this vision was that I could put my hobby away and ignore it when I had finished playing with it! The thought of not having to clean out smelly cages, feed dozens of hungry little mouths or worry over sick animals further encouraged me.

My father had been collecting and operating several gauges of electric trains for many years. Although I appreciated and enjoyed my dad's trains, I did not feel ready to tackle a multi-gauge train collection. What I needed was a fairly simple and enjoyable toy train that would still offer substantial play value for my children and me. Recalling a visit to my dad's home in 1977, I remembered seeing some large and colorful European trains — that my dad called LGB — running, of all places, outside on his lawn and patio. This was my first "close encounter" with LGB.

Bearing all of these memories and circumstances in mind, I took my wife by the hand and set off for the nearest toy store that I thought would most likely carry LGB.

LGB was for me. I would sell my exotic reptile collection and buy trains! A substantial amount of the wind was removed from my sails when we discovered that LGB commanded a rather stiff price: most sets sold for nearly $400 at that time and there was no action without a $40 transformer! A little discouraged but undaunted, we retraced our steps a bit. I recall muttering to myself as we drove home that perhaps my snakes weren't so bad after all and that we could go to K-Mart and pick up a Tyco set on sale for $19.95. My wife, however, whose brilliance is only exceeded by her good looks, offered one of those enlightened suggestions that come when I feel all is lost. She said, "Why not call your dad?"

Somehow, in my exuberance, I had forgotten that the most obvious way to solve our (my) problem was to "ask Dad." I called him immediately and he provided no less than six European and domestic sources for LGB. Upon examining the mail order price lists of the domestic dealers, I found that I could save quite a bit of money in buying from them; however, at that time European dealers were selling LGB for prices below those asked by any of the American sources. For example, the standard 20301 passenger set that retailed for $400 was available through German dealers for about $160. Although there were substantial savings offered by mail order buying, there were, also, as I was soon to discover, a number of drawbacks; the greatest disadvantage was time. If the items ordered were in stock, domestic mail order took from about five to ten days. European deliveries had to be paid for in advance and arrival took from two to six weeks. Problems relative to damaged or lost items were not easily resolved and U.S. Customs occasionally levied a duty on shipments. Nevertheless, I began placing small orders with the German dealers and, with the exception of some occasional damage, found the service to be fairly reliable.

The trains were fantastic and fulfilled my dreams. It wasn't long until some of my friends noticed how elegant LGB looked and what fun these trains were to operate and began placing orders with me for sets, track, buildings, etc. Before I realized what had happened, I was ordering several thousand dollars worth of merchandise each month and had created a business generated entirely by word of mouth. Within six months I started looking for a place to open a store! By now I had sold my reptile collection and had made enough money over the 1982 Christmas season to purchase a sufficient inventory for a small store. Almost overnight my new hobby had become a successful, thriving business.

GENESIS OF THE PRICE GUIDE

Once in business and seeing the large amount of LGB that passed through my shop, my trained taxonomic eye began to pick out variations in the equipment. I took great interest in and began discussing and raising questions about these variations with several friends who were considered old-time collectors. Some of these collectors supplied me with early catalogues and occasionally let me see their older LGB items. Their reluctance to share their LGB was not due to their dislike for me, but was rather because their collections were usually hidden away to emerge only at Christmas time. As I began to spend more time evaluating my new hobby, it became clear that a study of LGB variations would probably be well received, particularly since this was an unusual opportunity to get a grip on this line as it was being produced. The primary concern

voiced by most LGB collectors was that a tremendous amount of variation seemed to appear in the same items from one production run to the next. I discovered, as I scrutinized this issue and each production run, that occasional minor variations (i.e. the position of a decal or painted marking) could probably be attributed to the artistic license of factory personnel. Factory sanctioned changes generally took the form of new decals or painted decals — black stripes added to the 2060H locomotive — or an altered color — the 4041 hopper car was changed from red to orange. Minor variations in color were most likely caused by a casual mixing of paint, using different types of paint or changes in the pigments used to color the plastics.

Bearing all this in mind, I determined that the best way to define "variations" was to focus on consistent and more easily recognizable variables such as whether or not an item was painted, had frame markings, had a particular body type, etc.

After several months of studying, analyzing and chasing down variations and hard-to-find pieces, I finally assembled a rough but fairly complete manuscript. I mailed copies of the manuscript to several friends and associates in the LGB Model Railroad Club as well as dealers who had been carrying LGB since its early manufacture. To my surprise and delight the guide received very favorable reviews. With the reviews came information on additional variations and refinements. The book was really beginning to take shape and I was getting more and more excited about it every day!

While attending the fall 1983 TCA meet at York, Pennsylvania, I bumped into Linda Greenberg and told her about my endeavor. Linda liked LGB and was interested in the book. She asked to see and evaluate the manuscript. I realized at that moment that if the guide had any merit this evaluation would be the test.

As I look back, it doesn't seem like such a hurdle now, but I really thought I would strip my gears while the Greenbergs gave my "whim" the acid test. When I finally heard Linda's voice on the telephone telling me that she and Bruce were very pleased with the rough draft, I breathed a long sigh of relief. What I didn't realize was that lengthy prepublication revisions, changes and additions, etc., would take about twice the time it took me to assemble and write the original draft. What further complicated matters was that Lehmann was producing a considerable number of new, limited run items at the same time I was revising the manuscript. Although it seemed as if something new appeared just as I was getting the guide wrapped up, this circumstance gave me the opportunity to evaluate and catalogue many new items and variations just off the assembly line.

Although I organized and described the trains, had it not been for the help and advice of many good friends and colleagues, I would undoubtedly still be sitting behind a word processor in some darkened room wondering if the guide or myself would ever see the light of day. Avid LGB fans such as Rudi Enners, Robert Cage, Carter Colwell, Al Rudman, Joe Hylva, Dave Watts, Robert Schuster, Gary Keck, Howard Banzaff and Dan Jansen provided me with information and items to help keep me in stride with variations and changes made by Lehmann. Joe Hylva's **LGB Checklist** was a great benefit as well. My dad, Leonard Ottley, whose patience with me is most appreciated and still pretty good, inspired and motivated me to complete this endeavor.

PRICING

The one issue that caused me more headaches and will most likely never be completely resolved is pricing. Although most prices reflect genuine values from known sales, many items had to be evaluated according to their relative availability. In other words, some items are rare, but no one we knew had sold any lately, or an engine was hard to find, yet no one else seemed to be aware of it. For example, hot goodies such as the early green and white 2034 steeple-cab locomotive or the gray 4040 oil car, may fetch as much as $500 each. They are "rare," but the earliest dark green and black 2050 tramway engine, perhaps the rarest early locomotive, should command a value at least equal to that of the 2034 or the gray 4040, but it is known to have sold for only a fraction of their prices. Also, age should not be the primary dictate of value. Many recently produced transition pieces — items produced while a major color or detail change was occurring — are very uncommon. I have seen collectors pass over the rare but newer brown 4010 low-sided gondola with black and white markings or the orange 2033 service engine with gold plating on the manufacturer's plaque for an older yet more common piece.

In 1984, when Lehmann cut their prices to the American dealers by forty percent for new merchandise, many older items and transition pieces had their potential values masked by the devaluation as well. Due to these circumstances, I personally believe that many of these items, particularly the transition pieces, will soon command higher prices than the values listed in this guide. The pre-1973 items currently bring some of the highest prices; however, as collectors begin sorting out the variations from the mid to late-1970s more and more pieces will hit the "hot" list.

Perhaps the change that had the greatest effect on the LGB market was not Lehmann's production of some new or exotic locomotive, but rather their substantial price cuts of 1984. Their action was heartily lauded by LGB enthusiasts in the United States since they could buy the trains stateside at prices very close to those of the European mail order houses. The meager price differences between European and American mail order houses no longer justified the time it took to buy or the risk of damage from overseas purchasing. The price drop also made LGB more reasonable to buy in quantity and consequently more hobby shops and toy departments began carrying it. However, price has had very little to do with LGB's success. Quality and beauty are the keys.

Now, LGB's remarkable popularity has brought with it higher quality, lower prices and finally this new collectors' guide. Most people find that enjoying toy trains has a direct relationship to their self-expression, and LGB has that universal appeal that makes a person's involvement with toy trains a very desirable activity. LGB has cultivated a hobby. It has, as well, more simply, brought many would-be train nuts out of the closet. Whether you have a full-blown backyard layout or a circle of track on your family room carpet, you have already added to your vocabulary of fun — a language easily understood by owners of LGB.

WOLFGANG RICHTER AND LGB IN GERMANY
By Carter Colwell

At the snap of the switch and with much chugging, a large electric model of a steam locomotive comes out of the back wall, its shrill European whistle outlining the curve of the bar before it slows to a stop before me.

"I just use that to bring in drinks when we are having a meeting here," says Wolfgang Richter, co-owner and chief executive officer of the Lehmann Patentwerk. But we are having only a quick cup of coffee as we talk of the company's postwar development and Herr Richter's part in its growth; the open freight wagon is empty today.

Over our heads is a fifteen foot long clear plastic tube with a strange track and on it a low-wheeled mechanism hugs the rails. An experimental model propelled by magnetized track (linear induction), it was developed by Herr Richter's late brother Eberhard in hopes that it might prove to be a marketable item; but analysis showed production costs would be too high. Only the prototype was ever made, a dream that turned out to be impractical.

The walls around us and around the conference table behind us are lined with showcases. Silhouetted against the light-washed wall behind them stand all the current models of the largest mass-produced model trains in the world: LGB, the Lehmann-Gross-Bahn. Tens of thousands are produced at a time, for these are a dream that turned out to be practical indeed.

Perhaps the most famous toy makers in the world, the Lehmann company entered the period of World War II under the direction of Wolfgang Richter's father, Johannes. Already in his sixties when the war began, Johannes Richter refused to turn his toy factory into a war machine, and would not make military supplies. Although production fell radically, he managed to get some tin sheet until 1944 and to continue limited sales through Switzerland. When the Russians swept over Brandenburg, they went through the factory with naive delight, conscripting samples probably to be sent to their children in the USSR.

But though the Russians liked the toys, the East German government did not like the enterprise that made such a private success. Johannes was arrested for having too many employees. Held for four days, he could not be found indictable on any pretext, particularly not for military production, and he was released. But the Brandenburg days of Lehmann were doomed, and in 1948 a writ of expropriation was apologetically delivered by a civil servant who said he could see no legal basis for it. The factory was now "people owned," a Volkseigene Betrieb. Seventy years old in 1949, Johannes Richter brought his wife and three of his children still behind the Iron Curtain out of East Germany to Nuremberg.

"Nuremberg is the center of the toy industry," Johannes said, and he would consider no other site for a new beginning, although some of his future competitors were not too pleased to have the Lehmann name move into competition, even without capital, equipment or staff. And as competitors, their fears were justified. Poor but free, Johannes gathered his family to rebuild Lehmann. "These are the best conditions we have ever had," he told his sons. He must have been right.

They started working in the back yard, producing a small string-pull top. Wolfgang and Eberhard sold it from tables in department stores. The repair of a bombed building, the acquisition of a few old foot-operated machines and after a half year, a 20,000 Deutschmark line of credit, and Lehmann had begun its ascent. The credit was possible because Johannes Richter brought out of East Germany something the government could not expropriate — his good name. A reference from the co-founder of the Nuremberg Toy Fair convinced the local bank to make one of the best investments of the postwar period. The Richter family knew how to turn dreams into profitable realities. "Make toys," the old man told his sons. "The money comes later."

By the end of the 1950s, with the death at age 74 of Johannes Richter, the company was in the control of his two sons Wolfgang and Eberhard.

The toy business has always been a family activity for the Richters. Wolfgang remembers how as children they would go to the factory with their father on Sundays, and how impressed they were with the big rooms where the toys were assembled. He has written a description of the factory's source of power, transmitted through leather belts to drive all the machinery.

"The showpiece of the entire operation, as well as the main attraction for us, was the 'Lokomobile.' This machine generated the power for the entire factory, making it independent of the city power supply. The black, steam-driven monster behind the windows of the engine house was waited upon by the stoker, Mr. Lorenz, who sometimes let us climb the iron ladders to the various platforms, where we could admire the many polished brass levers, handles, fittings, oilers and the glittering movements of the piston-rods. I will never forget the unique mixed odor of coke, oil, grease and steam! The Lokomobile looked like an immense, walled-in express train locomotive to me. The only difference was that the wheels on this locomotive were on the top rather than the bottom."

At the end of the 1930s, of course, there did not seem much prospect for careers in the toy business. The foreign market was practically gone, the local market not much better. Wolfgang's oldest brother became a doctor, his oldest sister became a dentist and his other sisters married a banker, a teacher and a patent attorney. When the war had ended, as his father struggled to keep the factory in Brandenburg, Wolfgang was in Munich, working for the U.S. Army and taking night classes.

Although the company had solidly re-established itself, in 1963 it seemed stymied in a closed market without room for expansion. As tough and occasionally unscrupulous oriental competition constantly threatened to undersell with a sometimes inferior, sometimes stolen, but always cheaper toy, Wolfgang turned back to his childhood.

He remembers how as children they were bundled into two train compartments, shared with their parents and piles of luggage, by their governess Nina. (Johannes named a toy for her, a cat catching a mouse.) The occasion was their annual rail pilgrimage to a vacation spot on the Baltic Sea. The steam

This smallest LGB locomotive is powered by catenary wire and easily moves through its outdoor setting.

9

engines were exciting, and of course Wolfgang had to have a train of his own, a tinplate windup engine, green and black. He wanted to play with it at times in the garden, but dew and damp are bad for tin; and he had to be careful not to step on the tracks.

Perhaps inspired by his toy-building father, Wolfgang loved to build transport models — sometimes a ship or a plane — carved from wood. He designed them himself, working from photographs and plans. His brothers and sisters would play with the finished products.

One he remembers well was an engine, similar to the current LGB 2010. It was an old four-wheeled steamer with a straight stack, and was nearly the same size as the big LGB trains are now. Of course, it had tracks, made of strip wood held to wooden ties by glue and nails. (Wolfgang wanted, even as a child, toys that were sturdy and would last.) There were crossings and buildings and switches — hand-operated, of course. Wheels were a problem for the boy. So Wolfgang went to the factory during a noon break and without his father's knowledge asked a man in the shipping department, where cases were made of wood, if the cratemaker could help him. He could, and on his lathe turned rimmed wheels to put Wolfgang's childhood dream on the track.

In 1963 Wolfgang was himself a father. His son Rolf, who is with the company now, remembers clearly how Wolfgang designed models of toys for the kids to play with. In 1963 Wolfgang made a cardboard model of what would five years later be an LGB train. Rolf recalls that a nice thing about the big train (the model was redone several times, in wood, then in cut-and-glued plastic) was that you could use other toys with them, compatible for play even though not perhaps exactly to the same scale.

It took Wolfgang two years to convince his brother that a new line of trains, bigger than anything currently on the market, would be good for the company, two years of designing, redesigning, seeking motors and arguing. Eberhard saw, rightly, that the company would have to expand to handle a complete line of such magnitude, and by consent both brothers had to agree on a line of action before it became company policy. Eventually, he was persuaded. The line would be unique: Marklin and Bing had made No. 1 scale trains until the 1930s, but since then the trend had been toward smaller and smaller trains. First O, whose 1 to 48 scale ratio makes it about half the size of Lehmann's G scale 1 to 22.5, then in 1935 HO scale — "half O" — with its 1 to 87 scale, and since World War II N scale, 1 to 160, and even Marklin's Z scale, 1 to 220. Smaller, smaller, smaller. But LGB would be big.

LGB would be big enough to use with other toys. It would be tough. The trains and cars would be tough enough to run out of doors, unfazed by weather. The material would be tough, a tough plastic fused with fiberglass or rubber, and if the public needed to be educated that these were not cheap oriental plastics, it would be done. The track would be tough, tough enough to stand on. The track would be No. 1 size, a familiar size from prewar years, one that old trains could run on. The track would be narrow gauge, so that engines could run on tight radius curves small enough to use indoors as well as out, and still look realistic. It would, in the German tradition of toy trains, be a complete system, one that could be added to, changed, modified daily if one wished, giving way to shifting fantasies at will. And as that dream of variety is satisfied by the customer, the maker who satisfies the urge to novelty will not have to retool completely. Clever design of standardized

parts will see to that.

These considerations convinced Eberhard. The secret was closely guarded when the decision was made in 1965 to produce and market LGB trains. Three years later, in 1968, a prototype engine and two cars were on display at the Nuremberg Toy Fair. On the single-sheet flyer, as on subsequent catalogues in these early years, Rolf and his brothers play happily with the toy trains they tested.

The line is everything the Richter brothers wished. It is tough enough to run in snow; I have run mine in the rain. It is tough enough to run 8,400 hours, the longest presently known and proven endurance run; at the University of Ulm, an LGB locomotive is in the process of running mileage equivalent to a trip around the world, some 40,000 kilometers. The only question is whether the motor will hold up. As for the track, catalogue pictures proudly show not a child, but an elephant standing on it. The tight curves look fine with narrow gauge equipment, the 2040 model of the Rhaetian "Crocodile" locomotive, articulated in two places, looking good even when its twenty-two long inches negotiate twenty-four-inch radius curves. All LGB models, says Wolfgang Richter, even the new two-foot long Swiss passenger car just moving from prototype to production as this is written, will always be designed to operate even on the smallest curves.

"Elephant-proof" track!

And it is variable: not only in the layout flexibility of any sectional track, but also in the variety of equipment Lehmann will continue to offer. A circus train will follow 1985's first circus car; a cog locomotive is in the works; a "babyhead" cement car is in prototype and, as is appropriate in a line whose largest customer in a 40-percent export business is American, more models of American equipment will follow. And to the simultaneous delight and frustration of the avid collector, there are unplanned and unrecorded color variations caused by changes in the colors of plastic pellets and paint, even from the same supplier.

From time to time, models are discontinued. But the original little 0-4-0 locomotives will go on forever. "What if a time comes when there are no plastics, as some predict?" "Then we will do something else," Herr Richter answers. "But there

The black and red O-4-OT locomotive, brought from East Germany, welcomes everyone to the LGB factory.

will always be trains and people who love them."

Wolfgang Richter's dream of a toy train has become a practical reality. Automatic molders work twenty-four hours a day making "sleeper bed," tough brown plastic tie strip with tie plates, spikes and wood grain cast in. 12,000 pieces of curved track (catalogue number 1100) are made each day, all year long. Compressed air hisses from the automatic parts injection molders, as plastic pellets are heated, pressured into the molds and cooled with water. The recent expansion raised the number of molders from 10 to 40. Although production hours are 7:00 AM to 4:00 PM (to 5:00 PM during overtime runs), the automatic parts injection molders run from 6:00 AM to 10:00 PM.

An occasional metallic clank comes from the shop where a dozen craftsmen work on molds sometimes weighing more than half a ton. Twenty-six pairs of high quality steel molds will produce the new Swiss passenger car. By a new electric process, "erosion" machines burn small details into the molds with high voltage.

On three parallel tracks, mostly old aluminum rail, stand 74 dark green, colorfully-lettered baggage-mail wagons, ready for inspection. Soon they will be boxed and crated for shipment, pink labels decorated with an open umbrella and a wine glass slapped on each side of the package. The umbrella means "keep dry" and the wine glass means "fragile: this side up."

A worker welds the two red and white parts of a passenger car door together sonically, thereby leaving no surplus glue. Painting is by hand spray, the surplus automotive paint dissipating into a booth the size of a small room, with a foot of water in the bottom.

Each year, the factory makes two to three runs of every one of some 500 items in the LGB line. 12,000 of the new American prototype locomotives have been ordered in 1985, but only 10,000 can be run before 1986 in spite of the expansion that has doubled production.

The plant itself is a practical dream, a pleasantly asymmetrical group of boxes like a pile of Christmas presents. The Nuremberg city fathers were loath to assent to its bright red and white-banded colors, but finally agreed. "After all, it is a toy factory," Wolfgang Richter says crisply, walking through the overpass connecting two buildings separated by a street with a quick brisk stride that occasionally shuffles a little as though he is leaning too far forward and must step into the tilt of the earth to keep climbing it. Workers are breaking for lunch, and he exchanges "Mahl essen" greetings — "have a good lunch" — without pausing. The plant is increasingly automated, "Robert the First" being the latest robot, which as I watched removed a car body from a mold, placed it down beside others and clipped off the flues by which it had been held. But most of the assembly work is by hand, women's skilled fingers deftly slipping parts and screws together. Occasionally design calls for particular mechanical ability in assembly; Herr Richter thought it inappropriate to tell me what the assembly workers call the clerestory roofs of the 3010, 3011 and 3012 cars, with their recalcitrant roof frames, window sills and glass panes. These do not go together easily.

But constant improvement is the goal and the practice of the Lehmann Company, and the history of the product is a history of continual betterment. I commented on how ingenious the assembly of the 2010 locomotive was, and how cleverly parts were used to hold each other together, and Herr Richter replied it was too complicated. Next year, replacing the motor will be much simpler.

Experts, of course, work on the design of cars, locomotives, track, signals, translating the brothers' designs into practical actuality, into things that can be made for a price that can be paid. Every Monday morning the foremen meet with the owner, to suggest procedural improvements. The basic production practices established by Eberhard continue in effect. Recent improvements in production include new mold making machines and improved printing. Color separations, when masking is necessary, offer a possibility for color bleeding at the mask part-line; but an inspector stands ready, narrow paintbrush in hand, to touch up irregularities — by hand.

Decisions are influenced by the experience of users. When an early polystyrene faded, it was abandoned as a production material. For further color regularity, models are now painted, even though the plastic of which they are made may be the same color. The very first locomotives had spur gears; customer comments on the noise made by 10,000 revolutions per minute led to a change after seven or eight months to the worm gear motors now used. Foremen, customers, all contribute their insights to LGB management decisions, as do those in the sales network. For example, American importer Bill Lamping suggested the popular American caboose, 4065, and the Railway Express car.

Even the real trains on display outside the factory are subject to playful improvement. Rolf, soon to be joined in the family business by his cousin, Eberhard's son, has installed a smoke maker in the old black and red 0-4-0T locomotive brought here from East Germany. Now its stack smokes and its cylinder blow-down valves leak steam.

Herr Richter considers the decision to start again in Nuremberg their most important decision. Close behind that comes the decision for which he was so much responsible, the decision to produce LGB, now some 93 to 94 percent of their total operation. Important, too, were the decisions to produce in plastic and to sell directly to retailers, still unusual in the German toy industry.

Obviously, these decisions were the right ones. This family product appeals to families. Some say it should be called "Lehmann Gesundheit Bahn" — Lehmann Health Train — for the therapy of its indoor and outdoor play. The backbone of the clientele is fathers in their thirties, their forties and their fifties. Children love the trains. At adolesence their interest turns elsewhere, but when they start families of their own, they come back to them. Although train toys are traditionally masculine, women like LGB and suggest purchases. And age is no barrier to interest, as is shown by the material sent in to the "LGB Despeche" by an 89 year old New Zealander.

Where does the business sense come from, the practical know-how, that makes such success possible? Wolfgang Richter thinks it came from his experiences in Munich, in part, where he worked in an American Army clothing shop and learned about displays, stockkeeping and accounting. A good teacher at school (a German high school similar to an American college) taught him much about graphics. The basics of metal work he learned as an apprentice with a manufacturer of sterilizers and household goods who, during the material shortages of the postwar years, made tricycles for his employees out of such primitive materials as tin can covers.

Rolf Richter thinks his father does not adequately credit his own brilliant sense of layout and eye-catching design.

To one of the men who works with him, Wolfgang Richter is a down-to-earth person who wants quality first; the profit goes into tooling and expansion and new lines. (Here Wolfgang surely is his father's son: "The toys first; the profits come later.") Wolfgang Richter, says his staff, makes what is in his heart. And in his heart is a toy train.

PACKAGING
By Donna Price

LGB trains and accessories were originally packed in gray boxes with light red LGB logo and train insignias. In 1971(?)

those boxes were replaced by bright yellow ones with red and white logos and green train insignias. The bright yellow boxes were used until 1977 when red boxes with green and yellow logos and white train insignias were introduced.

Nearly all of the packaging material, from 1968 until the late 1970s, was composed of a simple two-piece folded and stapled carton and lid.

The one item that sometimes is damaged during delivery is the coupler. A packaging improvement Lehmann introduced at some point was a folded, stapled ring of cardboard, forming a tough cylinder (with squared corners) about one and one/half inches wide, one inch high and one inch deep to slip over the coupler hook.

In the late 1970s, some pieces, e.g., the Lowenbrau 4032L Beer Car, were packaged in yellow boxes with a plastic display window. Since these window boxes had inserts with wheel slots to keep the cars from moving in the box and end sheets with cutouts for the couplers, the protective cylinder for couplers was no longer needed though still used in most cases.

Red boxes with display windows began to appear at about this time too. These window boxes are slightly smaller and are made of lightweight cardboard. More recent versions are of corrugated cardboard and offer considerably more protection than their earlier counterparts.

Some experimental packaging apparently was used in the late 1970s in the form of an all clear plastic box with opening end tabs within a gray sleeve. Inside the plastic box was a 5/8" high cardboard base with a green stripe around the perimeter. A yellow tab and the Lehmann logo were printed on the stripe. The top of the base was printed in black and white with a picture of track and ballast. The top of the rail was highlighted in yellow. The bottom side of the base was printed in yellow with green and yellow logos. The one-piece base had only one end panel, printed in yellow, with the LGB sticker depicting the contents. (Some early stickers did not depict content; Roth comment.)

The Lehmann Company appears at this time to be switching almost exclusively to the red display window boxes — at least for rolling stock. This red is quite different from the 1977-1980 boxes. This packaging is attractive and promotes in-box display, and with cardboard inserts and supports, in addition to foam padding, it provides more protection than the earlier two-piece box. It also eliminates the staple scratches commonly seen on early pieces. If further strength of packaging is desired, an unlettered, plain gray cardboard sleeve surrounding the window box may be used for shipping.

Several Primus pieces are packaged in all-yellow boxes with display windows and sleeves. The ends have either an orange and white Primus label, or a Primus number stamped directly on the box.

EUROPEAN MEASUREMENTS

Measurements for all LGB equipment are given metrically. Both engines and rolling stock are reported in millimeters and reflect the length over buffers. (On real railroads buffers are knob-like protrusions at each end of the car, over or beside the coupler, which serve as powerful shock absorbers. They provide a flexible link between tightly coupled cars and prevent railroad workers from being squashed while manually coupling or uncoupling cars. Buffers also minimize car end "fishtailing.")

Chapter I
Train Sets

See specific sections in text for appropriate descriptions of variations of items found in each set. Other train set combinations may also occur due to manufacturer or dealer substitutions. Most sets were originally packaged with twelve sections of 1100 curved track (aluminum indoor track in earliest versions of all early sets), 5016 cable and a power pack (either 110V or 220V). However, many sets shipped to the United States had the power packs removed by the dealer/distributor since most had the 220V version not suitable for use with the American 110V standard, and the harder to find 110V power packs did not meet UL approval. In 1984-1985, UL approved power packs became available. The larger sets also came with the 5040 figures, 1052 uncoupler, 28 1150 track clips (locks), a catalogue, 0024 instruction manual and a subscription blank for **DESPECHE**. Beginning in 1983 copies of this magazine were also occasionally included in the packaged train sets.

300: 1980-86 railway starter pack with battery-operated 207 locomotive, plastic track and automatic switching; 4044 light railway wagon loaded with barrels; 3041 summertime passenger coach with bench seats, grab-handles for Playmobil figures. **CP**

3097: 1986, three blue "Orient Express" 3064OE passenger cars. The matching locomotive, to be sold separately, will be a 2071OE with white cab and blue tanks. **CP**

TOP: Set 20301BZ, the "Blaue Zug" (hence "BZ") or "Blue Train", also comes labeled in French. It was one of the first special trains to follow the 1981 anniversary set, issued in 1982-1983, and originally intended for European markets only but was first marketed in the United States by F. A. O. Schwarz. The window frames are red, an unusual color for frames, that matches the red frames and lettering of car 1982 (a supplement to the Lehmann Jubilee Anniversary Set).

CENTER: The Pinzga Schenke set, 20520, is the only limited edition set modeled after an authentic train; it is also the only limited edition passenger set to feature cars of a different color. Note the profile of the two roof vents on the middle car, a diner. The rectangular vent with rounded corners on the cab roof is typical of all 0-4-0T locomotives since the very earliest. Apparently the plaque says "Modellbahn Center", a hobby shop special.

BOTTOM: Set 20401RZ. The prototype "Furka" railroad comes by its "Oberalp" name honestly, as it goes over two alpine ranges, passing a glacier en route. "RhB" on the tank car stands for "Rhaetian Railway", the larger system to which the FO belongs. The car markings and warnings on the late model tank are typical of the increased lettering of recent LGB productions; very early cars had none at all. A. Rudman Collection.

13

TOP: Set 20501 (1984-1985), one of several numbers reused by Lehmann after the original item had been out of production a while; this is one of only two sets with the unique 4042 crane (the other is 20522). Note that the two cars are here coupled hook to hook, which the more flexible newer couplers facilitate; many operators add an extra hook at the loop end, to de-polarize coupling. The bulbous Baldwin stack identifies the locomotive as one of the 2020 series.
CENTER: The darkly dramatic 20517 has two identical 4003P container cars sporting the cartoon character "Commander Rom". "Videospiele" is video play or video game. Note the thinness and downward slant of the late model uncoupling pad.
BOTTOM: Set 20512 is pulled by a 2061FO. The Furka-Oberalp is part of the mountainous Rhaetian network, the largest European narrow gauge system, in southeastern Switzerland. The convivial burghers on the boxcar are, of course, quaffing Cardinal beer. Note the large roof ventilators. The newer angle iron railing on the 4034 brakeman's platform has no side gates. In ordinary service, such cars are operated with the brakeman's platform toward the front. A. Rudman Collection.

19801 BTO: Raffle set, custom painted for LGB Big Train Operator's Club (not painted by Lehmann); consists of 2095 engine painted orange with black stripe and "LGB" on sides; one standard livery 3062 and two 3063 coaches also with body painted orange with black stripe; black roofs and chassis. The set was raffled in a suitcase-like box with a handle and foam cushioned pockets for protection. A man from Pittsburgh won the set, and later sold it. J. Hylva Collection.　　　　　　　　　　**NRS**

20150: 1985, shown in 1985-86 catalogue and supplement 0011N; anniversary train to commemorate 150 years of German railways; "150 Jahre Deutsche Eisenbahnen" with red 2010DB or 2020DB locomotive and 3150(A) and 3150(B) coaches; approximately 2,500 sets were made. (NOTE: Companion car catalogued as 3150(C).)　　　**285**

20301: 1969-86, basic passenger set with 2020 locomotive, two coaches.
(A) 1969-70, 2020(A) locomotive, 3000(A) and dark green 3010(A) coaches.　　　　　　　　　　　　　　　　　　　　　**NRS**
(B) 1971-74, 2020(B) locomotive, 3000(B) and green 3010(B) coaches.　**NRS**
(C) 1975-78, 2020(B) or (C) locomotive, 3000(B) or (C) and green 3010(B) or (C) coaches.　　　　　　　　　　　　　　　　　　**NRS**
(D) 1977-78, 2020(C) locomotive, red and white 3011(C) and blue and white 3012(C) coaches.　　　　　　　　　　　　　　　　**NRS**
(E) 1979-82, 2020(C) locomotive, red and white 3011(E) and blue and white 3012(D) coaches.　　　　　　　　　　　　　　　　**185**

(F) 1983-86, 2020(D) locomotive, red and white 3011(F) and blue and white 3012(E) coaches.　　　　　　　　　　　　　　　　　**CP**

20301BP: 1984, uncatalogued; Buffalo Pass, Scalplock & Denver RR passenger set with 2076BP or red and black "B.P.S.&D.R.R. — The Roger T" 2076 locomotive, two barn red 3006BP or red "Buffalo Pass Scalplock". Only 2000 of these sets were made and only for the United States market.　　　　　　　　　　　　　　　　　　　　　　**385**

20301BZ: 1982-83, uncatalogued "BLAUE ZUG" blue train passenger set with dark blue 2020BZ(A) or (B) locomotive, two 3007BZ coaches.
(A) 2020BZ(A) (silver boiler front) locomotive.　　　　　**275**
(B) 2020BZ(B) (gold boiler front) locomotive.　　　　　**350**

20301MF: 1984, uncatalogued; Marshall Field & Company passenger set with 2020MF (a green and black 2020 locomotive), two dark green 3007MF "Marshall Field" coaches. The 3007MF coaches are also available separately. Only 500 of these sets were made for Marshall Field department store based in Chicago, Illinois.　　　　　　　　　**585**

20302: 1971-74, passenger set with green and beige 2034 steeple-cab locomotive, green second class 3008 or blue and white second class 3012 or third class green 3040 coaches.　　　　　　　　　　　**NRS**

20401: 1969-86, basic freight set with 0-4-0T locomotive, gondola and boxcar. (The make up of the older 20401 sets was varied; eventually 4020

TOP: Red, white and orange stripes camouflage the staid boxcar lines of this 4030 in set 20513, proclaiming "Spare Time/Hobby/Play". The passenger car is one of the 3007 series most often used by Lehmann in special livery sets. Its wider, squarer windows and Medium-Arched roof contrast to the narrow windows and Low-Arched roof of the 3000 coaches below it. CENTER: Set 20701DC has its little 2075 locomotive laden with a railroad name as long as itself, even when abbreviated. The letters stand for Dodge City and Great Western Railroad. The absence of valve rods (added to 2076D), which control steam flow in the prototype cylinders, is theoretically reasonable: many side tank engines carried such rods out of sight between the wheels. BOTTOM: Set 20301MF, which comes with a 2020MF engine, was issued for the famous Chicago department store, Marshall Field & Company, in a rich green with the company's founding year, the date of set issue and the company shield in gold. This set shows a 2010D engine not a 2020MF. The long vertical funnel right behind the front driver, typical of well-tank engines, represents just that: a funnel for filling the water tank. A. Rudman Collection.

was dropped because of the trouble of having two colors of the same car. C. Colwell comment.)

(A) 1969-75, 2040(A) or 2040(B) locomotive, straw brown 4020 or green 4021 gondola and straw brown 4030(A) boxcar. **NRS**

(B) 1975-76, 2040(B) or 2040(C) locomotive, green 4021(A) gondola and yellow "Chiquita" 4033(A) boxcar. **NRS**

(C) 1977-82, 2010(C) locomotive, green 4021 gondola and yellow "Chiquita" 4033 boxcar. **250**

(D) 1983-84, 2010(D) locomotive, 4021(E), (F) or (G) gondola and 4033(G) boxcar. In late 1984 some of these sets were issued with a 2020(D) locomotive. **250**

(E) 1984-85, same as (D), but with dark brown 4021(H) gondola. **235**

(F) 1985-86, same as (E), but has 2020(E) locomotive. **CP**

20401RZ: 1984, uncatalogued; "The Red Train" (Der Rote Zug), special freight set to promote the Lehmann company; with 2061 locomotive, red 4003RZ(A) container car, red 4040RZ tank car.

(A) 2061(B) locomotive. **275**

(B) 2061(D) locomotive. **200**

(C) 2061(E) locomotive. **200**

20501: 1969-74, freight set with 2060 locomotive, gray 4001 flatcar and green 4011 (listed, erroneously, as 4010 in 1970 catalogue). The differences between this set and 20501L are that at least the earliest of the 20501 came

with no light on the 2060 locomotive, and all came with indoor (aluminum) track. **350**

20501: 1983-85, uncatalogued, Vedes Company limited edition train set; includes 2020 locomotive, medium brown 4021(G) gondola and yellow 4042 crane car.

(A) 1983-84, has 2020(D) locomotive without factory installed smoke unit. **225**

(B) 1985, has 2020(D) locomotive with factory installed smoke unit; box has words "Mit Dampf". **250**

20501F: 1983, Florsheim freight set with red 2090(C) locomotive, white 4032F boxcar and brownish-red 4065F caboose; peel-and-stick decals. Production limited to 300-500 sets; J. Hylva comment. May also have been packaged in 20401 boxes. Reportedly, the set was made by LGB distributor Bill Lamping, of Milwaukee; B. Roth comment. **250**

20501L: 1971-78, "Junior" freight set with 2060 locomotive, 4001 flatcar and 4011 or 4010 low-sided gondola and aluminum or brass track. 1976 set came with chrome-plated track, A. Rudman Collection. White foam box with "LGB Junior" photo on lid in 1976. See corresponding years of cars in each car section of text for specific variations found in the 20501L sets.

(A) 1971-74, 2060Y(B) locomotive, gray 4001 flatcar and green 4011 low-sided gondola. **425**

(B) 1975-76, 2060G locomotive, gray 4001 flatcar and green 4010 low-sided gondola.   **NRS**

(C) 1977-78, 2060Y(C) locomotive, gray 4001 flatcar and green 4011 low-sided gondola.   **NRS**

20502: 1982, uncatalogued, Freizeit Hobby Spiel, "FHS" limited edition train set; includes 2075(C) locomotive, 4003F container car (erroneously dubbed 4002/69) and 4002(A) cable car with green spools; 1000 sets made.
                                                            NRS

20512: 1983-84, uncatalogued limited edition Furka-Oberalp "Cardinal Beer" freight set with 2061(C) (red and black diesel locomotive), yellow 4034(A) (with "4031" I.D. number) boxcar for set and medium brown 4010FO flatcar. 2000 sets made; B. Roth comment.   **250**

20513: 1983 or 1984, uncatalogued; Freizeit Hobby Spiel limited edition train set with red and black 2020HS locomotive, red 3007HS coach and red 4030 boxcar. 1,000 sets made; B. Roth comment.   **385**

20514: 1983, uncatalogued; "DHS SPIEL & HOBBY" limited edition freight set with 2020(E), 4003D container car (has 4069/1D container) and medium brown 4021(G) high-sided gondola.   **235**

20515: 1984, this is a non-factory set put together by a distributor in California. The only consistent item in the set was a 2020(E) locomotive supplied with a cowcatcher (from the 2017 locomotive) to be attached by the customer; the cars for the set could be chosen by the customer on the basis of 300 mm rolling stock that would fit in the box. The 20515 label on the box

was printed separtely and glued on over the factory-printed number 2020(D) and packaging, no cars.   **165**

20516: 1983, uncatalogued; Brinkmann Company limited edition train set; includes 2020(E) locomotive, green 4021(G) gondola and 4033B boxcar.
                                                            400

20517: 1984, uncatalogued (correct number is 380.7030); "Commander Rom" limited edition freight set for the Philips Video Game company; with 2060P locomotive, two midnight blue 4003P container cars with randomly scattered heavenly bodies on the dark background. Box reads "Philips GMBH Videospiele Romzug Komplett"; 4003P container car has space robot figure, with "Commander/Rom" written on white shirt front; blast burst reads, "Videospiele/von Philips". 1,000 sets made; B. Roth comment. Approximately 150 of these sets were independently repainted with the Pennsylvania (Pennsy) road name in both Tuscan red and Brunswick green versions for the North Coast Distributors, Ohio.   **250**

20518: 1984, uncatalogued, Einkaufsring limited edition train set (also numbered 20518EK); includes red 2061 diesel locomotive, brown 4021(G) gondola and orange 4041(E) hopper car.   **NRS**

20519: 1984, uncatalogued, freight set "Einkaufsgemeinschaft" with 2076D locomotive, orange 4011 hinged-hatch wagon and orange 4041 hopper car. A Rudman Collection.   **185**

20520: 1984, uncatalogued; "PINZGA SCHENKE" Austrian railway train

TOP: Set 20526 is a railroad jubilee set for the E. Otto Schmidt Bakery in Nuremberg. The red Schmidt logo, a heart with some of the castle-like towers of Nuremberg on top, appears on the chocolate brown container just left of "Schmidt-Lebkuchen". "Lebkuchen" is a German variety of spice cake. The set's boxes are numbered from one to 1,000; collectors disagree as to how important the numbering is.

CENTER: Black and orange set 20519 is only one of many dramatic color combinations possible with LGB. The little 0-4-0T, a 2076, carries its water in side tanks (the square boxes beside the boiler) instead of in a well tank underneath the boiler, like the other two engines, above and below it.

BOTTOM: Set 20514 pulls a high-sided gondola used for more general purposes in Europe than here, and a 4003 car with a container labeled "DHS Play and Hobby". A. Rudman Collection.

set with 2010PB (green and black 2010 "Pinzgauer Bahn") locomotive, dark green 3007PB (green 3007 "Modellbahn Center Sonderzug") coach, dark blue 3013PB diner (blue 3007 "Pinzga Schenke" bar car with 3013 interior). (NOTE: Less than 100 sets imported into the United States; exact number of sets manufactured is not known.) **425**

20522: 1984, uncatalogued, Freizeit Hobby Spiel "FHS" limited edition train set; includes 2010(E) locomotive with dark brown cab, 4002(D) cable car with green spools, and 4042(E) crane car. **NRS**

20526: 1984, Schmidt Bakery Freight set in dark brown with 2010SB locomotive, 4003SB (brown "Schmidt Lebkuchen aus Nuremberg" 4003) container car, 4030SB (brown "Schmidt Lebkucken aus Nuremberg") boxcar. (1000 sets were made, the boxes numbered sequentially, the train items themselves not numbered.) **300**

20528: 1985, uncatalogued; "150 JAHRE DEUTSCHE EISENBAHN", Modelleisenbahn Schweiger (Schweiger Model Train Shop) anniversary passenger set to commemorate 150 years of German railways; with 2020MS(A) or (B) (yellow and black "Schweiger" 2020) locomotive and two 3007MS(A) (yellow "150 Jahre Deutsche Eisenbahn" 3007) coaches. Only 1000 sets made, numbered on bottom of engine. First 60 sets have locomotives 2020MS(A) (black unpainted boilers) a few of which were only available for sale through Modelleisenbahn Schweiger; some of these may have had the boiler fronts painted silver. 60 percent of these sets have been

in the United States. As of May 1985 Mr. A. Muller (store owner) advised that this set will not be reproduced; J. Henderson comment.

(A) 2020MS(A) (black boiler front) locomotive. **500**
(B) 2020MS(B) (gold boiler) locomotive. **400**
(C) 2020MS(C) (silver boiler) locomotive; reader comments requested. **NRS**

20529: 1986, uncatalogued; green-painted 0-4-0T locomotive (either 2010 or 2020) and two 3007MS(B) coaches (complete description pending release of set); set sold without track or transformer. **385**

20531A: 1985, uncatalogued, Abele Company limited edition train set; includes 2020MF(B) locomotive and two silver 4003A container cars. **NRS**

20531B: 1985, uncatalogued, Breuninger Company limited edition train set; includes 2020MF(B) locomotive and two chocolate brown 4003B container cars. **425**

20531CS: 1985, uncatalogued, Capri-Sonne limited edition train set; includes 2020MF(B) locomotive and two royal blue 4003CS container cars **425**

20531DV: 1985, uncatalogued, Dauth Company limited edition train set; includes 2020MF(B) locomotive and two silver 4003DV container cars. **NRS**

20531K: 1985, uncatalogued, Kurtz Company (of Stuttgart, West Germany) limited edition train set; include 2020MF(B) locomotive and two yellow 4003K container cars. **NRS**

TOP: In Set 20532 the most distinctive feature of this livery, celebrating a Berlin landscaping company, is the casual irregularity of the child-like flower drawings. Contrast the minimal profile of the three roof vents with the sharp spindle profiles of the paired vents in the set below; both kinds are typical of recent issues of their respective car types (3007, 3000/3006).

CENTER: Set 20301BP clearly appeals to an American market, both buffalo and scalplocks being European rarities. Cars with Simulated Wood sides (3000/3006), rather than the Simulated Metal of 3007, were probably chosen for the same reason. Not sold in Europe.

BOTTOM: As a model train shop in Nuremberg, Schweiger had Set 20528 issued to celebrate the one hundred fiftieth anniversary of railroads in Germany. The cars feature the old locomotive "Der Adler" ("The Eagle"), Germany's first, between the Jubilee year dates. On the engine cab door, the clever "150" logo of the railroad exposition, which was held in Nuremberg, is arranged to suggest a steam locomotive with long stack. A. Rudman Collection.

20531KT: 1985, uncatalogued, Kenner Trinken Wurtemberger limited edition train set; includes a 2020MF(A) locomotive and two silver 4003KT container cars. **400**

20531L: 1985, uncatalogued, Lindau limited edition train set; includes 2020MF(B) locomotive and two silver 4003L container cars. **NRS**

20531MC: 1985, uncatalogued, Modellbahn-Center (Schuler Company) limited edition train set; includes 2020MF(B) locomotive and two royal blue 4003MC container cars. **400**

20531P: 1985, uncatalogued, Panne Company limited edition train set; includes 2020MF(B) locomotive and two silver 4003 container cars. **NRS**

20531S: 1985, uncatalogued, Schinacher Company limited edition train set; includes 2020MF(B) locomotive and two silver 4003S container cars. **NRS**

20531SF: 1985, uncatalogued, Schnabel Company limited edition train set; includes 2020MF(B) locomotive and two silver 4003SF container cars. **NRS**

20531TS: 1985, uncatalogued, Sindel Company limited edition train set; includes 2020MF(B) locomotive and two silver 4003TS container cars. **NRS**

20531Z: 1985, uncatalogued, Zinthfner Company limited edition train set; includes 2020MF(B) locomotive and two silver 4003Z container cars. **NRS**

20532: 1985, "Bundesgartenschau-Express"; made for a landscaping company in West Berlin, it consists of a green and black 2020(E) locomotive and two dark blue-painted 3007BE passenger cars (with yellow stripe and "Bundesgartenschau Express-Berlin 1985" markings). The 3007 is deep blue with gold line and corner decorations; four windows with orange-yellow window frames and "BUNDESGARTENSCHAU-EXPRESS" over two center windows. "Berlin", "1985" with child-like flowers between the two. Black chassis. Black filigree brackets; six ribs to roof, three vents on every other section; roof tinted from black at outside to medium gray along most of roof top. Interior has five sets of medium brown bench seats on a blue floor. **250**

NOTE: There were supposed to be 1000 sets made, but 400 of the sets had a misspelling on the coaches and were destroyed, leaving only 600 sets for sale; J. Hylva comment. A. Rudman thought that only 500 sets were manufactured.

20575: 1976, "Junior Steam" freight set with 2075 steam locomotive and aluminum track; B. Cage comment. **NRS**

20601: 1974-75, black 207 battery-powered locomotive, with two bright yellow 4044 high-sided wagons. **125**

20601: 1979-82, goods train basic set with 2075 locomotive and two 4043 tipping bucket cars. **125**

20601B: 1977-78, battery-driven goods train set with 207 locomotive and two orange-brown 4044 high-sided wagons. **NRS**

20601L: 1975-76, same as 20601; but with people for Playmobil. **NRS**

20601T: 1977-78, same as 20601; but with transformer. **NRS**

20602: 1983-84, Platelayer's starter set with 2075 locomotive.
(A) With red and white 3041 excursion car and red 4043 bucket car. **125**
(B) With red, grey and white 3041 excursion and yellow 4044(C) ore car. **155**

20675: 1975, "The Big Ore Drag" freight set with 2075 steam locomotive and aluminum track. Authenticity of this set is questionable. **NRS**

20701: 1979-82, passenger train basic set with 2075 locomotive and two red and white 3041 excursion cars. **125**

20701DC: 1982, uncatalogued; Dodge City and Great Western RR set made for the LGB National Sales Distributor in Milwaukee, Wisconsin. Set comes with 2075DC locomotive and two yellow 3006 coaches in first and second class. Because some of these coaches had 3000 identification

numbers they were wrongly dubbed by some collectors as 3000DC; however, the factory designated these coaches 3006. 2,000 sets made; B. Roth comment.
(A) 2075DC(A) with red drivers; 3006(A) and 3006(D) coaches. **300**
(B) 2075DC(B) with black drivers; 3006(B) and 3006(E) coaches. **250**

20701T: 1977-78, same as 20701 above, but in earlier packaging. **200**

20801: 1981, catalogued in 1984-85 with additional cars; red 100th anniversary "Jubilee Train" set for the Lehmann company, with red 3007LJ coach and red and white 3013LJ diner. Original sets uncatalogued and marketed at about half the cost of an ordinary set, but have escalated in value more than any other; 10,000 manufactured, W. Richter comment. Additional cars manufactured to go with this set: white 1982, blue and white 1983, blue 1984 and blue 1985. Price does not include extra cars.
(A) With 2010LJ(A) locomotive. **900**
(B) With 2010LJ(B) locomotive. **1100**

20801B: 1981, 207 (green, battery-powered) locomotive, with one pinkish-red 3041 (C) 170 mm excursion car and one orange-brown 4044(B) 150 mm high-sided gondola with pale blue Aral barrels.

380.7030: See 20517.

The very earliest of set 20501, with a 2060 locomotive had no headlights. The gray 4001 was common to all issues of the set, but the 4010 shown here was sometimes substituted for a green 4011; the 1975-1976 catalogue shows a brown gondola with the set. Although the 1970 catalogue lists 4010 (brown), while showing a green car, the downward slant to the uncoupling pads means these cars are 1974 or later, and most probably the set was listed in 1975-1976.

Chapter II
Steam Locomotives

The nostalgic appeal of the steam locomotive affects even those who have grown up in the age of diesels and electrics. That popularity is reflected in the much larger number of steam locomotives, compared to the other types, in the Lehmann roster. In the Centennial Catalogue of 1981-1982, for example, eleven standard run steam locomotives are listed, seven diesels and five electrics. When the handmade locomotives are added, all of which are steam, the disparity is even greater.

STANDARD PRODUCTION STEAM LOCOMOTIVES

The models of the 0-4-0T (B-h2 and B-n2) conventional tank locomotives are probably the most well known among LGB enthusiasts and are perhaps the engines most responsible for Lehmann's success. Since the water and coal supply of a tank locomotive is not sufficient for long trips, a tender is added when needed with the coal normally stacked in front and the water stored to the sides and rear (as in 2015D). NOTE: The German "tenderlokomotive" translates to tank locomotive in English, while a "schlepptenderlokomotive" is a locomotive with separate tender. Lehmann's models of these little engines have excellent tractive power, reliability and versatility.

The earliest versions of these locomotives have a relatively bland appearance when compared to those more recently produced and, owing to their noisy drive mechanisms, have been affectionately dubbed "grinders" or "growlers." The "grinders" are noisy because they are driven by the 2100 motor with a spur gear on the single drive shaft. (These spur gears changed after seven or eight months, although the motors continued to be available as catalogued replacements for some years; W. Richter comment.) However, some locomotives with spur gears were available as late as 1971.

Over the years cosmetic as well as mechanical improvements have been made. Most early versions are entirely unpainted and have less detail than newer versions. Examples are:

1. Early smoke box doors, until about 1971-1972, lack simulated latches on the right side, and the forward portion of the boiler lacks rivet heads.

2. The sand dome on early models lacks the round side plate and lever as well as the actuating rod along the boiler into the cab. Oval peel-and-stick manufacturer's labels, colored red and gold, are positioned at the base of the sand dome on early versions, but were moved about midway up the sand dome when the round plate and lever were added to the later versions. Some of the earliest locomotives may not have had peel-and-stick labels; J. Barton and C. Colwell comments.

3. On later models, beginning about 1974, three additional embossed piping details were added to the side of the boiler.

4. The wheel-shaped latch handle on the smoke box door and the small round valve handles on each side of the boiler, directly beneath the sand dome, are black on locomotives until about 1981. On subsequent models these handles have a gold finish.

5. On early models the small box atop the boiler, directly in front of the sand dome, lacks all detail and has smooth corners. This box on later models (beginning about 1974) has simulated angle irons on the corners and rivet-head details. Smoke box

rivet detail and roof detail added with square roof vent; J. Barton comment.

6. The snowplows on early models differ slightly from those of newer models. Newer snowplows are notched to better clear the position of the couplers.

The large size of the taillight and the white ring around the oval buffer help identify this as a late model steamer. A. Rudman Collection.

7. The buffers of early models are rectangular. More recently, oval-shaped unpainted buffers replaced the rectangular ones. The latest models have oval-shaped buffers with white edging. The white edging was painted on the prototype buffer borders in later years as a safety feature. It enabled the worker between the cars to see the outline of the buffer plate better at night; D. Weiler comment.

8. The earliest models, from 1969 to perhaps 1971, may totally lack gold finish on the window frames, the embossed numbers and the "LGB" letters on the cab.

9. Earliest versions from 1969 to 1970 or 1971 have a small round knob-like cab vent on the roof. This cab vent was replaced by a slightly larger, squared-shaped version on later models.

10. Very early versions may lack lighting altogether and have only unlit lamp units. The operating head lamps on locomotives produced from 1969 to about 1970 are less than 13 mm in diameter. Later versions have bezels (rings or frames around the lens) with a 20 mm diameter. Concomitant with the change in head lamp bezel diameter was the introduction of a reversing lighting system, one in which the head or tail lamp glows according to the direction of travel.

11. Locomotives with the early 2100 motors with spur gears lack 2210 pickup shoes as do some of the models up to about 1971.

NOTE: New lighting sockets for facilitating coach lighting were phased into production in the mid-1970s, first being mentioned in the 1976 catalogue. This is a most important feature and can be helpful in establishing the era of a particular locomotive.

Early locomotives of all series had small loops on their rear couplers, not interchangeable with the present coupler and incompatible with cars having double end hooks, which cannot make a tight turn; the engine hook will jam the car hook inside the small loop.

U-locomotives 0-6-2T (C1-n2t) are modeled by Lehmann after the versions built by Lokomotivfabrik Krauss & Co. for 760 mm gauge railways. These versions weighed about 24 tons and could achieve a maximum speed of 35 to 45 km/h.

This unusual combination for 0-6-2T-series locomotives of two steps high on the side of cab and tank, an early feature, and grate-less rear windows, a late feature, can probably be dated 1979. A. Rudman Collection.

The LGB models have several minor characteristics that may be used to distinguish early and later models. All early versions (2070, 2071, 2072, 2073) until about 1979 have two

staggered steps protruding from the left side of the water tank and cab toward the forward half of the cab. These versions also have four horizontal grates over the rear cab windows, except for the 2070 which has only two because of the placement of the coal bin. Later versions have only the rear step and lack the rear window grates. Steam generators are absent from the earliest versions, but appear on most models as of 1973.

An early 2070 has a red plastic trailing wheel and somewhat low cab roof. Although the lower roof is prototypically accurate, it was modified in response to customer complaints about how it looked with the taller rolling stock. A. Rudman Collection.

Early versions have disc-type drivers and red plastic trailing wheels, although the disc-type drive wheels appear to have been used at least until 1980 or 1981, after the plastic trailing wheels were discontinued and replaced by metal tire plastic trailing wheels with electrical pickup.

The head lamp bezels on the front of the water tank on the early 1971-1973 models may have been shallower than those of the more recent models. A more definitive observation is requested.

Early versions of the 0-6-2T series have a distinctly shorter cab height than current versions; produced after 1977 since the earlier cab height was shorter than the roof lines of the boxcars and coaches. This change made the locomotives more esthetically appealing at the sacrifice of prototypical accuracy.

To describe railway stock in terms of wheel arrangement, use is made of a code:

Code 1, 2, 3 means numbers of idlers.
Code B, C, D means number of linked drive axles (A — 1, B — 2, C — 3, etc.)
Apostrophe means such axles are swivel mounted in main frame of locomotive to enable it to master tight curves.
O means the wheel-set group has individual drive.
In other countries, designations of wheel arrangements correspond but in most cases numbers are used. A locomotive with wheel arrangement C'C' would be, for instance, 6/6 in Switzerland, 6-0-6 in France and 0-6-6-0 in America. In America, the number of wheels is given, not axles. The type 1'B1' is a 2/4 in Switzerland whereby the number 2 denotes the number of driven axles and the 4 is the total number of axles. In America a 1'C would be 2-6-0.
As an example, consider the C'C-n4vt wheel arrangement designations:

The triangular, straight-line coupler hook identifies this 2010D as a non-current model, although the picture appeared in the catalogue as recently as 1985. Comparison of individual pieces of gravel with that in earlier catalogue photos of the same locomotive confirms that this picture was taken — and the locomotive therefore made — by 1979. Curved hooks replaced the triangular one, and plastic web springs replaced the metal coil spring just visible in the photo, ca. 1980. Catalogue pictures are not proof the model shown was still being produced in that configuration.

C'C means Steam locomotive with two power units, the first of which is flexibly mounted, with three drive axles each.

n4 means saturated steam and four cylinders.

v means compound action between high and low pressure cylinders.

t means fuel and water supplies carried on locomotive. In cases where the "t" is omitted the engine involved always is a tender locomotive, while a "T" means locomotive without a tender. Most of the LGB locomotives will have a "T" following the American wheel classification implying a tank-type locomotive without a tender; C. Colwell comment.

206: 1974-75, see 207.

207: 1975-86, B-n2 class (0-4-0T) tank locomotive BR 995001 of the German State Railway. Battery-powered unit very similar to the 2075 locomotive but with a medium green or dark green unpainted boiler and tanks; black cab; red chassis; drive wheels are cast in red plastic. Engine originally produced in shiny black plastic, red underframe and wheels; no traction tire or traction tire on one rear wheel. In early catalogues, locomotive actually numbered 995001, with white letters. (It also has a boiler front number plate which is blank; no embossed numbers; D. Doggett comment.) **CP**

2010: 1968-86, B-n2 class (0-4-0T) tank locomotive, modeled after an 1898 vintage Austrian locomotive from the Salzkammergut Local Railway SKGLB, Salzburg-Bad Ischl. Straight standard stack, total length equals 250 mm. See comments above for brief history and detail variations.

(A) 1968-86, unpainted black boiler and green cab; cab window frames; embossed "LGB" on sides of cab and framed "1" on sides and back of cab

lack gold leaf; dull red chassis, early boiler and cab details (see comments on page 19); black valve and lock handles on boiler; small head and tail lamp bezels with non-reversing lighting system; engineer in left side of cab; black whistle; rectangular buffers without white edging; early 2100 spur-drive motor, no pickup shoes or traction tires.   **175**

Partly in response to the comments of American Charles B. Small, author of numerous books on narrow gauge lines around the world and of the first "Model Railroader" article on the new scale, Lehmann very early introduced electrical pickup shoes or skates on all its 0-4-0Ts. The shoe, attached by a screw, slides on its rail between the two drive wheels.

Looking like a European's idea of an American locomotive, with its European wheel arrangement, cab and tender Americanized by diamond stack and cowcatcher, 2017D nevertheless has an authentic prototype. Appropriately, it is a locomotive made by a German company for export to America. Like the model locomotive, the model tender has its own motor.

(B) 1971-73, same as (A), but with gold-finished cab numbers only; worm-drive; pickup shoes. **165**

(C) 1974-76, similar to (A), but with gold-finished cab numbers, window frames and embossed "LGB" on cab; 2200 worm-drive motor and 2210 pickup shoes; traction tires. **150**

(D) 1977-82, same motor and pickup shoes as (C), with dark brown-painted cab; improved, larger, reversing head and tail lamps, clear front lens, red tail lens; oval buffers without white edging; engineer in left side of cab; brass-colored whistle. Some cabs may have been painted a light green; V. Winn comment. **125**

(E) 1983-85, same as (D), with white "Letzte HU.26.6.79" on front of chassis, brass-colored valve and lock handles on boiler. **CP**

2010D: 1969-86, same as the 2010 with a 2010/2 smoking stack added and has the following variations:

(A) 1969-70, same as 2010(A), but with smoking stack. **NRS**

The 2015D, a tank locomotive with a tender added for longer runs, has a stack like 2017D but lacks the Americanizing features of that engine (cowcatcher, lantern headlight). C. Colwell Collection.

(B) 1971-73, same as 2010(B), but with smoking stack. **165**
(C) 1974-76, same as 2010(B) or (C), but with smoking stack. **165**
(D) 1977-82, similar to 2010(C) or (D), but with dark green-painted cab. **125**

(E) 1983-86, same as (D), but with white "Letzte HU.26.6.79" on front of chassis. **CP**

2010DB: 1985, same as 2010(E), but cab and boiler front are painted red with the "150 Jahre Deutsche Eisenbahn" lettering on cab; sold only with set 20150. See 2020DB for complete description. **NRS**

2010LJ: 1981, tank locomotive for the 100 year anniversary Lehmann Jubilee train set, sold only with the 20801 set; same basic locomotive as 2010, but has a cranberry-painted cab with gold-painted draped leaf chain and small "100 Jahre Lehmann" oval gold chain on cab door; black chassis; Baldwin-type non-smoking stack, oval builder's plate on dome.

(A) Red paint on cab is cranberry red with semi-gloss finish; smoke box door and boiler front beneath smokestack painted silver, gold vent door on side and boiler plate; raised "1" and "LGB" in gold in raised plaques on cab, engineer on right side. Buffers with white line. Price for set. **900**

(B) Red paint on cab may be slightly brighter and more glossy; smoke box door, boiler front beneath smokestack and front of chassis painted metallic red; engineer on left side. Price for set. **1100**

2010PB: 1984, uncatalogued; Pinzgauer Bahn Austrian, 0-4-0T tank locomotive similar to 2010(E); dark green-painted cab; no gold on cab numbers or "LGB"; small bronze-colored plaque on sides of cab with the words "Pinzgauer Bahn"; sold only with 20520 set. Price for set. **425**

2010SB: 1984, uncatalogued; 0-4-0T tank locomotive for the Schmidt Bakery 20526 freight set; very similar to 2010(E), but cab is painted a rich chocolate brown; sold only with set. Price for set. **300**

2015: 1975-76, B-n2T (0-4-0) locomotive with tender of the KPEV (Royal

Prussian Municipal Railway). Unpainted black boiler and cab; unpainted pinkish-red chassis; early non-smoking, funnel stack with spark arrestor; no KPEV eagle emblem or other markings on tender; early drivers; length 385 mm.

(A) Powered tender, brownish-colored coal load in tender, engineer in left side of cab. Some early versions lacked the jumper cable socket on the engine although the tender had both jumper sockets and geared axles ready for a second motor; B. Roth comment. **420**

(B) Unpowered tender, black-colored coal load in tender, engineer in right side of cab. **300**

2015D: 1977-86, same locomotive as 2015, with smoking stack and black coal load in tender; length 450 mm.

(A) 1977-78, locomotive cab and tender in medium green; tender has KPEV eagle emblem; early (disc) drivers. **355**

(B) 1979-82, locomotive cab and tender in black satin finish; tender may or may not have KPEV eagle emblem; Cooke-type 2015/3 smokestack; early disc or late spoke drivers. **CP**

(C) 1983-86, same as (B), with standard 2010/3 smokestack; late spoke drivers. **CP**

NOTE: Both early disc and spoke drivers have solid metal wheels with plastic simulators (either spoke or disc) inserted.

2016: 1975-76, United States Western-type 0-4-0 locomotive and tender with cowcatcher, based on engines used in Mexico, Canada and America (California and one excursion ride in New England). Medium green cab and tender with yellow striping; large yellow and black "LGB" on each side of tender; silver-colored boiler front with "6" front number plate; black chassis on locomotive and tender; early non-smoking funnel stack with spark arrestor; early black-spoked drivers; "2016" on bottom of locomotive between drivers; early engines did have jumper cable socket (cf. 2015(A) above); tender not powered; axles not geared; early red 2001/1 wheels; length 480 mm. Although this model is not listed in any catalogue, the photograph with the 2017 number in the 1977-78 catalogue is actually a 2016. This locomotive was actually patterned after a locomotive built in Germany for a German movie depicting the American West or an American "Western"; B. Schuster comment. Although there were no U.S. locomotives to appear such as these, they were modified to appear more "American" in an attempt to satisfy a growing demand for a U.S. prototype locomotive. **300**

2017: 1977-82, same basic locomotive as the 2016 but with a powered tender with black 2065/1 wheels; either early or late drivers; length 440 mm. **225**

2017D: 1983-86, same as 2017 with Cooke-type 2015/1 smoking stack; late drivers.

(A) 1983-84, red head lamp cowl plain, no painted filigree. **CP**

The 2018D locomotive, with its bulbous spark-catching stack and sturdy proportions, is Lehmann's first serious move into American prototype locomotives, although a number of American prototype freight cars (log 4066, box 4067, cattle 4068 and reefers 4064, 4070 and 4074) already existed. Demand outran production by over 20% in 1985.

(B) 1984-86, red head lamp cowl with yellow-gold filigree. **CP**

2018D: 1985-86, 2-6-0 Mogul tender locomotive similar to the type found on almost all narrow gauge railways in America and used especially for negotiating tight curves through narrow canyons and river beds. With non-powered eight-wheel tender painted dark green; red cowcatcher; black smoking balloon stack; black boiler front with silver door and yellow "18" on front number plate; red boiler; dark green cab and tender; length 665 mm. Although production was pushed back to 1985, a few pre-production prototype models and first-run pieces may have been imported into the United States in late 1984. Actually a D.S.P.&P.R.R. model although lettered D.&R.G.W. in the 1984-85 catalogue (cab and tender were also lighter green than production models). Production models have "D.S.P.& P.R.R." lettering. A decal set was provided to alter the road name on the tender to "Denver Rio Grande" or "D.&R.G.W." plus several engine numbers. When it was discovered that the boiler weight of the first run could shift and crack the plastic, a boiler-weight retaining screw, and, perhaps for the same reason, a second friction tire and a second screw at cab front (F. Pac comment), were added, to compensate. 10,000 Moguls were built in 1985, although 12,000 were ordered by September; C. Colwell comment. A model with a completely black boiler will probably be available in early 1987 and a sound version of this engine will probably come forth in 1987 with a proposed catalogue number 2018S.

(A) Shown in 1983-84 catalogue, "D&RGW" painted on sides of tender. Non-production prototype. **NRS**

(B) 1985, gold "D.S.P.&P.R.R." on sides of tender; no screw in cab front to secure weight and only one drive wheel with traction tire. **CP**

(C) 1985-86, same as (B) with screw in cab front to secure weight; traction tires on two drivers. **CP**

2020: 1968-86, B-h2 (0-4-0) "Stainz 2" modeled from an 1892 vintage tender locomotive of the Steiermarkischen Landesbahnen. Has Baldwin-type non-smoking stack; length 250 mm.

(A) 1968-70, unpainted black boiler and dark brown cab with embossed "LGB" and framed "2" in gold finish on sides and back of cab; red chassis, black whistle; smokestack lacks rivet-head and other details; small head and tail lamps with reversing lighting system; early disc 2010/1 drivers, rectangular buffers without white edging; early 2100 spur-drive motor and no pickup shoes. **190**

(B) 1971-73, same as (A), with gold-finished cab numbers only. **165**

(C) 1974-78, similar to (A), but with gold-finished cab window frames, framed "1" and "LGB"; 2200 worm-drive motor, 2210 pickup shoes; brass-colored whistle; large head and tail lamps, rivet-head and other details added to smokestack. Also available without gold-trimmed window frames; D. Doggett comment. **150**

(D) 1979-82, same as (C), but with medium green-painted cab; larger improved head and tail lamps with reversing lighting system. **CP**

(E) 1983-86, same as (D), with the markings "Letzte HU.26.6.79" on front of chassis; brass-colored valve and lock handles on boiler. **CP**

(F) 1985, same as (E), but has factory installed 2010/3 smoke unit; sold only with limited edition train sets 20501(B) and 20531K. **NSS**

2020BZ: 1982-83, 0-4-0T tank locomotive for the Blue Train, a limited edition set originally made for the European market which was later imported into the United States and gained great popularity; similar to the 2020, but has a royal blue-painted cab, a silver-painted boiler front and black chassis; Arabic "2" and "LGB" in gold, gold valve vent on side and valve circle on boiler front; sold only with set 20301BZ.

(A) 1982-83, uncatalogued; smoke box door and smoke box (boiler front beneath smokestack) are painted silver. Price for set. **250**

(B) 1983, uncatalogued; smoke box door and smoke box are painted gold. Price for set. **300**

2020DB: 1985. An 0-4-0T locomotive produced for the 150th anniversary of German railroading which was sold only with set 20150. The locomotive has a red-painted cab and boiler front, with gold plating on embossed number "2", "LGB" and window frames on cab; flat black-painted chassis and 2010/1 red wheels, gold-colored "150 Jahre" and "Deutsche Eisenbahn" below embossed "LGB" on sides of cab; "1832" and "1985" with multi-colored heralds (one is yellow with red and black stripes and a black eagle, the other is white with a green clover in the middle) are on the cab doors. **285**

2020HS: 1984, this tank locomotive came as part of the "Freizeit Hobby

Solid drivers with holes have been used on 2010 and 2020 locomotives from 1968 up to the present day, as on this special edition locomotive 2020HS; but only the earliest 0-6-2T series locomotives and the earliest 2075 have solid drivers rather than the current spoked ones. A. Rudman Collection.

and Spiel" limited edition 20513 train set; has a deep, shiny red-painted cab with orange, red and white horizontal stripes along each side of cab. Although these were made for the 20513 set some were sold separately in a blank box; J. Hylva comment. **150**

2020MF: 1984-85, uncatalogued, originally produced for the Marshall Field Company limited edition train set but was later included in several other limited production sets in both non-smoking and smoking versions; cab is dark green (same as 2010D(E)) but has embossed number "2"; all embossed markings and window frames in gold; red chassis.

(A) 1984-85, has standard Baldwin-type non-smoking stack; sold only with sets 20301MF and 20531KT. **NSS**

(B) 1985, has factory installed 2010/3 straight smoking stack; sold only with sets 20531B, 20531CS, 20531K, 20531L and 20531MC. **NSS**

2020MS: 1985, uncatalogued, "Schweiger Set" 20528 with 2020 tank locomotive; black boiler with black or gold forward section, gold boiler plate, bumper with white margin; unpainted yellow cab with typical dark olive-green roof with black weathering at edges; black vent on roof, raised "2" and "LGB" plaques, two olive-green horizontal stripes across cab (one just below the windows and one at the lower edge of the cab); "Schweiger" in half-red, half-black letters, beneath embossed "LGB" on each side of cab; black "150 Nurnberg — Furth 1985"; "150" logo on bottom of door; flat black-painted chassis and red 2010/1 wheels.

(A) Black, unpainted boiler front and smoke box door; some of these may have been repainted silver after leaving the factory. Reader comments requested. **NSS**

The square plate above the oval was added in 1972, after two years of production of 2070, the only one of the 0-6-2T locomotives to have no coal bin in front of the left cab window. A. Rudman Collection.

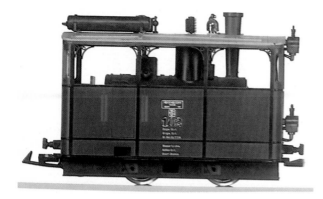

The 2050(A) steam dummy above is a rare color; the tramway locomotive's age is marked by the comparatively meager piping on the front half of the roof. Compare this photo with the one below.

(B) Gold-painted boiler front and smoke box door. **NSS**

NOTE: 2040 steam and 2040 electric, two different engines with same number.

2040: 1969-75, B-n2 (0-4-0) tank locomotive; modeled from a 1923 vintage industrial locomotive of the Siegerland Industrial Railway. Unpainted black boiler and cab, red chassis; earliest versions have small non-working head and tail lamps which were shortly thereafter changed to a non-reversing lighting system; narrow support ring around rim of smokestack; cab has embossed "LGB", "4" and window frame; gold finish, if present, usually on numbers only on sides and back; black whistle; no engineer.

NOTE: early catalogue photographs depict this locomotive without gold finish on embossed numbers or window frames. "4" embossed in plain

black, gold or silver. J. Hylva Collection.

(A) 1969-70, early spur-drive motor, no pickup shoes; no sticker, no lights, no gold except bell, no driver, cab has small, round roof vent. **400**

(B) 1970, same as (A), with black bell and reversing lights. B. Roth Collection. **350**

(C) 1971-74, same as (A), with worm-drive motor, 2210 pickup shoes, traction tire; may have reverse lighting. **350**

(D) 1975, same as (C), with square-shaped vent on roof; worm-drive motor; 2210 pickup shoes. **350**

2050: 1969-85, N-n2 (0-4-0T) tramway tank locomotive; modeled after the locomotive named "Feuriger Elias" of the Oberrheinische-Eisenbahn Gesellschaft (OEG). This unit, although called in America a "steam dummy," is a steam locomotive, but has flat slab-like sides and a gently curved roof so as to present a less menacing appearance to horses which share city streets with it. The model comes with green sides, a black boiler, black or red chassis and three head lamps but no tail lamps; length 255 mm. one of the last locomotives to get lighting sockets; B. Roth comment. Discontinued in 1985.

(A) 1969-70, body sides very dark green, not painted, with black-painted support seams; black chassis and wheel skirts; body has embossed manufacturer's and "OEG" plaques above "102" all in gold finish; roof is painted whitish-gray and lacks many embossed details found on later versions (i.e. the lack of a ring with rivet-heads at the opening in the roof where the smokestack passes through and a row of rivet-heads across the front of the roof). The roof also lacks all piping detail, including the steam pipe which passes throught the roof just anterior to the smokestack as seen on later versions. Window glass is flat and lacks the raised frame edging. Power supplied by the early 2100 spur-gear motor; also lacks 2210 pickup shoes and sockets for coach lighting plugs. The 1969-70 catalogue depicts this locomotive with only an "LGB" logo plaque on body sides in place of the above described plaques and numbers. However, the 1969-70 version was probably not produced in that exact form and the piece depicted may only be prototypical. The earliest catalogue rendering of this engine

The last cataloguing of 2050 was first produced in 1969 and discontinued in 1985. The earliest version lacked much of the last version's complex roof piping. The box-like housing of this late nineteenth century steam tram, covering boiler, firebox and rods, was intended to make it less frightening to horses.

Canted lids on the steam chests, above the cylinders, are one of the many European features of this 2070's prototype. On the model, well detailed opening smoke box doors were a feature from its introduction in the 1970 catalogue. A. Rudman Collection.

The two staggered steps on this 2072, one in front of the cab lettering and the other under the closed coal bin, are early characteristics. A. Rudman Collection.

(1969-70) is black and white and of little help in deciphering color or fine details. This version is probably one of the rarest early locomotives. **275**
(B) 1970-72, similar to (A), but body is lighter colored, being unpainted medium green with a black chassis and red wheel skirts; window glass has raised frame edging. **175**
(C) 1973-74, same as (B), but with red chassis. **150**
(D) 1973-76, similar to (B), but roof is slightly darker gray and has piping details including steam pipe passing through roof just forward of the smokestack; embossed roof details include ring with rivet-heads around opening in roof for smokestack and a row of rivet-heads across front of roof; 2200 worm-drive motor and 2210 pickup shoes; traction tire. **135**
(E) 1977-85, similar to (C), with body sides painted medium green (has a shinier finish than previous versions); some of the piping detail on the boiler is in gold finish; manufacturer's and "OEG" plaques on body sides lack gold finish; only the "102" number has gold finish; brass sockets for coach lighting plugs on the rear body panel. **125**

This coal bin at rear distinguished the 2070, first of Lehmann's series of Krauss 0-6-2T's, from other locomotives in the series. The smoking version, 2070D, was discontinued in 1978. A. Rudman Collection.

The long stacks of the old Lehmann steamers (here, 2072) were not always smokers, but they are always functional: ending in a long bolt, they pass through the boiler, often a lead weight, the chassis and the front coupler loop to hold the engine together. A. Rudman Collection

The colorful 2073D, green, red and black, has as its prototype a really colorful original preserved on a really narrow (760 mm) gauge, really short (13.6 km) line, the Waldenburg Railway. On special occasions, the locomotive runs through the placid valley of its Rhine tributary to feed the Swiss main line near Basel. The model's third headlight is a dummy.

2070: 1971-74, C-1 (0-6-2T) tank locomotive, U. 43 series of the Steiermärkischen Landesbahnen. With Baldwin-type smokestack, coal bin at rear of cab; dull black finish on boiler and cab; one step protrudes from left side of body adjacent to forward portion of cab and two grates are on each rear cab window; no steam generator is present on boiler.

(A) 1970, early version, non-smoking Cooke-type stack with early 2010/1 drivers, red plastic trailing wheels; oval manufacturer's plaque on sides of water tanks and "U. 43" plate beneath window of cab; lacks snowplow; head lamps mounted at top front of water tanks; engineer in cab, black rectangular buffers; cab lower than cabs of post-1974 models. A. Rudman Collection. Reader comments requested. **NRS**

(B) 1972-74, similar to (A), but with early 2070/1 drivers; additional

The steam generator between the dome and sandbox dates this 2072 with its distinctive closed coal bin in front of the cab, as post-1972; the metal wheels in the trailing truck also mean it is not one of the earliest. A. Rudman Collection.

rectangular manufacturer's plaque on water tanks; snowplow present; head lamps mounted on lower fronts of water tanks. **400**

2070D: 1972-78, same as 2070(B), but with smoking stack; length 340 mm. Last version made has red pin stripes like 2071D; B. Cage comment. **400**

2071: 1971, C1-n2 (0-6-2T) tank locomotive, U-series of the Zillertal Railway. Baldwin-type non-smoking stack, no steam generator; open coal bin in front of left cab window; dull black finish on boiler and cab; early 2010/1 drivers; red plastic trailing wheels; manufacturer's plaques on water tank and number plates located on cab; head lamps mounted atop front of water tanks; lacks snowplow. Reader comments requested. **NRS**

2071D: 1972-85, same locomotive as 2071, but with 2070/2 smoking stack; manufacturer's plaques located on cab; length 340 mm.

(A) 1972-78, similar to 2071, but with early 2070/1 drivers; 2070/3 smoking stack; head lamps mounted on lower fronts of water tanks; red chassis. **235**

(B) 1978-80, similar to (A), with red pin stripes on water tanks and cab; early type drivers; metal trailing wheels. **160**

(C) 1981-86, same as (B), with black chassis. **CP**

2071OE: Production due in 1986, uncatalogued; similar to 2071D, with white-painted cab and blue boiler and water tanks; gold graphics proclaim a limited edition model of the "Orient Express". **NA**

2072: 1971-74, C-1 (0-6-2T) tank locomotive, U-series of the Steyertalbahn; closed coal bin in front of left cab window; head lamps mounted on lower fronts of water tanks; boiler and cab in dull black finish; standard (straight) non-smoking stack and 2070/1 drivers only; length 340 mm.

(A) 1971, has markings "OBB", "298.53" and additional white numbers also on smoke box door; early type drivers; red plastic trailing wheels; rectangular buffers; no snowplow. **375**

(B) 1972-74, same as (A), but with snowplow; oval buffers; deep head lamp bezels. **350**

2072D: 1973-78, same as 2072(A) or (B), with smoking stack; length 340 mm. Metal trailing wheels from 1974; B. Roth comment. **365**

2073: 1973-74, (0-6-2T) tank locomotive, U-series "Eurovapor" of the Waldenburg Railway, the only line with a 760 mm gauge in Switzerland, branching off from the Swiss Federal Railways Basel-Olten line from Liestal to Waldenburg, a distance of 13.6 kilometers. Same boiler and cab configuration as 2072, with the addition of a third dummy head lamp above the boiler front and extra boiler details; cab and water tanks painted medium green, black boiler, red chassis; smokestack is the standard (straight), non-smoking variety; drivers are the 2070/1-type only; length 340 mm. Three reported made with light gray side tanks; C. Colwell comment.

(A) No markings or plaques on body; older drivers; red plastic trailing wheels; rectangular buffers; shallow head lamp bezels. Reader comments requested. **NRS**

(B) 1973-74, same as (A), with "298.14" on smoke box door and also on plaque in gold finish with the "Eurovapor" name located beneath cab window; oval buffers; deep head lamp bezels. **235**

2073D: 1973-86, same as 2073 with 2072/3 smoking stack in the following variations:

(A) 1973-78, same as 2073(B). **235**

(B) 1979-83, similar to (A), with fine yellow pin stripes on water tanks and cab; older or newer drivers; metal trailing wheels. **170**

(C) 1983-86, similar to (B), with slightly heavier yellow pin stripes; late drivers. **CP**

2075: 1973-84, B-n2 (0-4-0T) locomotive of the East German Railway, type number 99 5001, formerly Spremberg urban railway locomotive 11. Dull black-painted body; open coal bin at rear of cab; non-smoking stack and no lights; length 240 mm.

(A) 1973-?, boiler and water tanks in dark, unpainted very dark green; pinkish-red chassis; small black and gold metal "LGB" plaque. May also have been produced for the Primus Company; reader comments requested. **NRS**

(B) 1974, most detail markings in white, however the embossed letters of the Deutsche Reichsbahn plaque are in gold finish; pinkish-red or red chassis; early 2010/1 drivers. **100**

(C) 1974, similar to above with dark green-painted cab and water tank; LGB logo plate only marking on center portion of each water tank; possibly made for Primus. G. Mentiras Collection. **NRS**

(D) 1975-84, no gold finish on Deutsche Reichsbahn plaque; early or late 2015/1 drivers; usually with red chassis. **CP**

2075DC: 1982, same as 2075, but painted with Dodge City and Great Western Railroad logo "DC&GR. W RR" in white over "Little Billy" in black on curved yellow panel on tank side and "2075" in white on cab doors.

(A) Late 2015/1 red drivers. **125**

(B) Late 2017/1 black drivers. **125**

2076: 1983-84, same basic locomotive as the 2075, with dual head and tail lamps; brake hoses; extra boiler details; rear coal bins with working, hinged lids; interior light in cab; valve gear rods, with reversing rod and eccentrics; may have had a non-smoking stack. May not have been produced in this exact form. Reader comments requested. **CP**

2076BP: 1984, uncatalogued; similar to 2076D, but with red-painted cab; white-lettered "B.P.S.&D.R.R." and white pin stripes on sides of water tanks; "The Roger T." above "B.P.S.&D.R.R." above "2076" in white on cab doors, "The Roger T." in yellow on water tank and smoke box door; red chassis and cab steps; engineer figure in cab. Sold with set 20301BP and

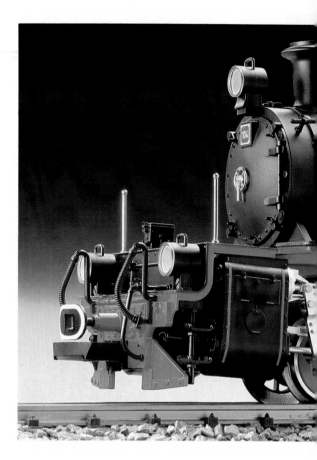

The 2076D's model ancestors include battery drives in several shades of green (207) and the black, track-powered 2075. Besides smoke, the newer version has acquired full external valve gear (rodding on the wheels to control steam flow into the cylinders), operating headlights and free-standing brake hoses.

though not originally sold separately, some sets were broken up, the locomotives reboxed and sold individually as were the cars; B. Miller comment. Some may have three-position switch; window glass and curtains in cab doors; D. Doggett comment, confirmed by J. Barton. **130**

2076D: 1983-86, same as 2076, with smoking stack, window glass, window curtains in cab door; "on-idle-off" switch inside cab. **CP**

(A) No engineer in cab. **CP**

(B) Engineer in cab. Sold with Set 20519. **NSS**

2080: 1974-76, 1'C1'-h2t (2-6-2T) tank locomotive built by the Krupp Company and used by the East German State Railways (Trans-Harz). Boiler and cab in dull black finish; red or pinkish-red chassis; although production models have a smoking stack, earlier versions or prototypes may have been non-smokers; length 410 mm.

(A) 1974, engine number "99 6001" on boiler front and beneath cab windows but only the cab numbers painted white; black cab step, forward step (in front of boiler) a single rectangular unit, steam generator stand is well over half as long as the steam generator itself; red plastic leading and trailing wheels; early 2080/1 drivers; probably a prototype. **NRS**

(B) 1975, engine number on boiler in white and additional white markings on saddle tanks and cab; red cab fore-step composed of two rungs; steam generator stand only one-half as long as generator; upper surfaces of forward deck unpainted pinkish-red; metal leading and trailing wheels; early 2080/1 drivers. **275**

(C) 1976, same as (B), but with upper surfaces of forward deck painted black. **NRS**

2080D: 1977-86, same as 2080, with smoking stack and the following variations:

(A) 1977-78, same as 2080(B), with smoking stack; "Deutsche Reichsbahn" in gold finish. **265**

(B) 1978-86, same as (A), but with white skull and cross-bones warning on sides of saddle tanks; early or late 2080/1 drivers. "Deutsche Reichsbahn" may not be in gold finish; D. Doggett comment, confirmed by J. Barton. **CP**

2080S: 1974-86, same as 2080 or 2080D, with electronic synchronized steam, bell and whistle sounds with the following variations:

(A) 1974-75, same as 2080(A), with sound; has mechanical bell. **NRS**

(B) 1975-76, same as 2080(B), with same sound as (A). **NRS**

Articulated locomotives, with their double drive mechanisms, are a visual joy in operation. Note the large front cylinders, operating in the prototype (preserved at the Blonay-Chamby Museum Railway in Switzerland) from partially expanded steam that has already been through the rear cylinders of this compound engine. The model hinges both mechanisms to accommodate the radically tight 1100 curves, whose 600 mm radius barely exceeds the 510 mm length of the locomotive.

(C) 1977-78, same as 2080D(A), with same sound as (A).   550
(D) 1978-84, same as 2080D(B), with same sound as (A).   550
(E) 1984-86, same as 2080S(D), with improved electronic bell sound and additional compressor sounds. Previous versions have a "clacky" mechanical bell while this version has a "clear ringing" bell sound. Compressor sounds are sustained and gradually taper off after power is removed.   CP

2085D: 1982-86, 0-6-6-0T (C'C-n4vt) mallet tank locomotive manufactured by AG Hanomag in 1925 for heavy duty use on steeply inclined stretches of track with numerous bends; used in service by the South German Railway Company (SEG). Boiler and cab finished in dull black paint with glossy, dark green saddle tanks; SEG logo and "104" on sides of cab, manufacturer's plaque on sides of saddle tanks, "104" on boiler front and additional markings and ZELL plaque on cab; smoking stack; 2085/1 drivers.

(A) Early prototype is a composite of two 2071D locomotives with two 2010/5 chassis; boiler and water tanks are flat black. Tested for factory by R. Enners for one year. J. Cooley Collection.   NRS
(B) 1982, smokestack tilted slightly forward due to problems with early boiler molds; flat black finish on boiler.   550
(C) 1983-86, smokestack normal, not tilted forward; boiler has flat black finish with lightning bolt warning decals on smoke box door, dome and rear of cab.   CP

HANDMADE LOCOMOTIVE SECTION

Brass handmade locomotives were manufactured by C. Hohne in limited numbers, a maximum of 100 each year, for LGB. All of these locomotives require LGB 1600 wide radius track (235cm) and 1605-1615 switches. All have reversing lighting.

1977L: South African Railways, 2-8-4 class 24 locomotive was designed for short line work. It was developed in 1949 from totally new technical concepts since the weight over the axles could not exceed 11 tons. The solution was to cast the frame and cylinders as one piece — a production carried out in Great Britain. Other weight savings were gained by using a Vanderbilt-type tender. One especially fine feature was the over-sized firebox which allowed the burning of low grade fuel. Tractive force equals 12,530 kg. Model length is 815 mm, height 154 mm, width 118 mm and weight 11.8 kg; powered by a Buhler 6-18v motor; locomotive and tender are lighted; number series 3601 to 3700.   6200

1978L: Caminhas de Ferro Mocambique, 2-6-2+2-6-2 Garratt-type locomotive is probably one of the best prototype locomotive designs and was patented in 1907. The two British companies, Beyer Peacock & Co. and Kitson & Co., made the greatest advances in this construction concept. This locomotive-type is in operation today in South Africa. Model length is 812 mm, height 157 mm, width 123 mm and weight 10.7 kg; powered by two Buhler 6-18v motors; locomotive is lighted front and rear; number series 2035 to 2134.   5700

1979L: Bridal Will Lumbering Co. (Bridal Veil) 2-6-6-0 mallet locomotive is one of the most widely used articulated designs. (Due to mis-translation, this locomotive was mis-lettered "Bridal Will" for the Bridal Veil, Co. of Oregon; D. Weiler comment. Over the years it has been refined and is virtually unrivaled for reliability and power. This style was first produced in the United States during the 1880s. In 1904 and later it was also found in South America. This model was operated on a private short line in Brazil and has a cabin tender. Model length is 790 mm, height 162 mm, width 113 mm and weight 10.8 kg; powered by two Buhler 6-18v motors; locomotive and tender are lighted; number series 201-300.   6400

1980L: Giradot Railway of Columbia, 2-6-6-2T Kitson Meyer mallet locomotive is actually a modification of the Garratt. (This type of construction allows coal and water to be stored directly on the engine, concentrating more weight over the driving wheels thus increasing traction.)

The husky 2080 was the first steam locomotive to be equipped with sound at the factory, including both chuff and mechanically triggered electronic bell. Introduced in 1974, the 2080S underwent a few minor variations in lettering. The skull and crossbones on the tank were added in 1978.

The design also allows the locomotive to operate on tight curves. The engine was very popular in Bolivia, Chile and Columbia, and most were produced by the British firm, Kitson & Co. Model length is 760 mm, height 135 mm, width 159 mm and weight 11.2 kg; powered by two Buhler 6-18v motors with lighting front and rear; number series 35 to 134. **6400**

1981L: Argentine State Railroad, 4-8-2 locomotive with condenser tender, was a promising innovation in locomotive design. It allowed operation in areas where water was scarce and greatly improved fuel consumption. This locomotive still operates in southern Africa and South America. The Henschel & Sohn Company is mostly responsible for the development of the condenser system through Dr. Roosen. Model length is 970 mm, width 128 mm and weight 11.4 kg; powered by a single Buhler 6-18v motor; number series 8001 to 8100. **6500**

1982L: Indian State Railway SR (Southern Region), 2-8-2 Micado-type locomotive with smoke deflectors amd standard tender. Approximately 5000 of these locomotives with various wheel arrangements and pulling capacities were supplied by Krauss-Maffei-Munchen, Henschel-Kassel, North British and United States companies as part of the Western Alliance Development Aid program. A number were also manufactured in Indian Railway yards under license. Some of these locomotives are still in service today. Model length is 875 mm, height 155 mm, width 140 mm and weight 7.8 kg; powered by a Buhler 6-18 volt motor in each tender truck, locomotive and tender are lighted; number series 6801-6900. **5500**

1983L: Tungpu Railway of China, 2-10-0 decapod locomotive which was originally produced by Krupp Locomotive Works in West Germany and in the 1930s was produced in the United States by Lima-Alco. The model is based on the German-built versions supplied to the Schansi province of China. This design was chosen due to small permissible axle load. These locomotives were very reliable and saw service up until the 1950s. Model length is 720 mm and weight 7.5 kg; powered by a single Buhler 6-18v motor; both locomotive and tender are lighted; number series 318-417.

4500

Chapter III
Electric Locomotives and Trolleys

These are the two longest lived steeple-cab electrics of the six originally issued. The blue and white 2030 was the first to be catalogued, in 1970; and with some modification in lettering and striping is still in production (see below). The other five colors were introduced almost immediately, in 1971-1972, but four of them were dropped after 1973-1974, and the red-bottomed 2032 continued only two years longer, through 1975-1976, perhaps retained because it matched the red-bottomed 3011. C. Colwell Collection.

The rapid drop from the Alps to the sea makes hydroelectric power practical in much of Europe, as does the dense population, reducing the distance over which power must be distributed. Even short lines are often electrified. Sometimes, when such lines merge, different electrical systems are maintained. On the Rhaetian Railroad, most of the system operates on single-phase alternating current at 11,000 volts, 16-2/3 cycles. (The Swiss standard gauge lines operate on 15,000 volts.) But the Chur-Arosa line in the Rhaetian network operates on 2,400 volts direct current. On European rails, electric locomotives thus are common and varied.

Lehmann introduced electric locomotives to its line in 1971 with a group of six virtually identical steeple-cab locomotives, differentiated by their color. They were numbered consecutively from 2030 to 2035, although two of those numbers, 2035 and 2033, would be used for quite different electric motors later, when the originals had been discontinued. Only the blue and beige 2030 was continued past the mid-1970s; it was still in production in 1986 in a slightly gaudier livery. 2030, 2032 and 2034 have two-toned finishes, with beige tops and blue, red and green bottoms respectively; 2031, 2033 and 2035 are solid blue, red and green. Judging from catalogue photos, the company had in mind the possibility of passenger trains in colors that

matched the engines, especially the two-toned ones, and featured such groupings in ads. However, only 2034 was ever issued with a factory set.

The early pantograph engines, 2030-2035, were produced from 1971-1974. They had internal wiring soldered directly to the motor housing, which made them difficult to disassemble. Later, screw contacts were introduced facilitating the removal of the cab from the motor housing, a principle used in other locomotives as well. All originally lacked lighting sockets.

Additional lettering and, since 1984, black pin stripes distinguish 2030E externally from its predecessor, the long continued 2030. Internally, it has the EAV electronically delay start, which means other locomotives can be run at slow speeds on the same circuit without moving the 2030E.

2030: 1971-82, electric "steeple-cab" locomotive AEG E1 1508 of the 10.4 kilometer long Mixnitz-St. Erhard Local Railway; modeled after the Bo class AEG electric locomotives built in 1913 and used mainly to pull a mixture of passenger coaches and goods wagons. Blue and beige body; solid colors unpainted; black chassis with red brake shoes and arms; red grab-irons; dark red pantograph; early versions lack lighting plugs; length 245 mm.
(A) 1971-73, no lighting plug   **165**
(B) 1974-82, lighting plug present   **125**

2030E: 1983-86, same as 2030 with EAV (electronic start delay) system. EAV units allow simultaneous shunting with a second locomotive on the same loop.
(A) 1983-84, same colors as 2030; silk-screened white lettering "GEW. Lok 15, t" over "P 10, t" over "Hd 8, t" over "H.-Unt. 0.0. 1984" (this last sequence may be a production date and it may vary from run to run) to the left of the cab door; "LuP 5, 09m" to the left of the last of the above listed marking sequences; raised portion of manufacturer's plaque on door same color as body; head lamps same as early models with bulbs protruding from lensless bezels; smooth roof.   **125**
(B) 1984-86, similar to (A), but with black pin stripes on beige portion of cab; black and white pin stripes on blue body (blue color slightly darker than an earlier version); "H.Unt. 6.6.84" as possible production date; head lamps have lenses which conceal bulbs; textured roof.   **CP**

2031: 1971-74, blue steeple-cab locomotive, same basic locomotive as 2030(A) of same railway company, but with body cast entirely in medium blue unpainted plastic.   **500**

2032: 1971-74, unpainted red and beige-painted steeple-cab locomotive, same basic locomotive as 2030(A) or (B); white lettering to the right of door reads "Lb. M.-st.E." and to the left of door, "Lup 5.09m / Gew. Lok 15 t / P 10, t / Hd 8. t / H.-Unt.0.0.1980". Has lighting plug, doors open in, gold-painted horn on left front, engineer inside.   **350**

2033: 1971-73, red unpainted steeple-cab locomotive, same locomotive as 2030(A), but body is all red. No lighting socket. The original issue, with no lead weights inside, does not have as good an electrical contact as the later, weighted models.   **550**

2033: 1977-86, B-class electric track maintenance locomotive, similar to those found throughout Switzerland and used for construction and repair work as well as branch line and tramway operation and shunting purposes with forward service platforms, large head lamp, small tail lamp, flashing warning lamps on roof; red 2030/3 pantograph; length 270 mm.
(A) 1977, unpainted green body; red chassis with yellow and black hazard marks at each corner; green roof insulators; no opening on left side of platform at steps; embossed plain, unpainted manufacturer's plaques and numbers; no tools or barrels on service platform. This version may never have been produced.   **NRS**
(B) 1977-78, similar to (A), but with unpainted medium green body; black roof insulators; open access on left side of platform at steps; embossed manufacturer's plaques with gold finish; embossed "60" on cab painted white; red and white or yellow and black hazard stripes at each corner.   **350**
(C) 1979-81, same as (B), but with medium green-painted body without gold finish on manufacturer's plaques.   **250**
(D) 1983, unpainted orange body; gray chassis; plain embossed manufacturer's plaque and unpainted "60"; EAV system.   **200**
(E) 1983-84, same as (D), but with embossed manufacturer's plaque in gold finish and "60" painted white.   **250**
(F) 1984, same as (D), but without gold finish on manufacturer's plaque.
                                                                                 200
(G) 1984-85, same as (C), but without embossed "60" on sides but rather a silk-screened "2033" with additional white dimension markings at lower position of cab.   **135**
(H) 1985-86, dual flashing lights on top, new power switch, slightly heavier than earlier models.   **CP**

The newer version of the 2033 work motor with platform, its number reassigned from an old steeple-cab, follows the recent Lehmann trend toward electronic sophistication. Body color changed from green to this orange in 1983, and in 1985 the single flashing rooftop light became two, their flash rate independent of locomotive speed.

After most of the 2030-2035 steeple-cab locomotives were discontinued, Lehmann reassigned some of the numbers. 2035 went to this typically narrow-bodied one-truck streetcar. The trailer has the same body but no pantographs or motor. The brown (rather than yellow) window frames mean these were not produced in the first two years, 1977-1978, but later.

2034: 1971-74, green and beige steeple-cab locomotive; same basic locomotive as 2030, but body unpainted green and painted beige. No lighting socket. **475**

2035: 1971-74, green steeple-cab locomotive; same basic locomotive as 2030, but body entirely unpainted green; red plastic grab-irons, gold-painted horn on left front side; black roof and black or red pantograph. No lighting socket. **525**

2035 (3500): 1977-86, conventional style yellow trolley car with enclosed driver's platforms; yellow and white-painted body; red 2030/3 pantograph. The 3500 trolley trailer has the same basic body as the 2035 but is unpowered, lacks a pantograph, has 3000/1 plastic wheels and sells for about 40 percent of the powered unit; both have two seated figures in illuminated passenger compartments; length 350 mm.
(A) 1977-78, yellow window frames in black supports on sides of body; no red tail lamp. **NRS**
(B) 1979-86, brown window frames; supports on sides of body painted black; non-illuminated red tail lamp present in early models. Working directional taillights in most; V. Winn comment. **CP**

2036 (3600): 1978-84, old-fashioned red trolley car of the kind used everywhere after the horse drawn era; with open drivers' platforms; three windows on both sides of car; red and white-painted body; black current collector bow. Working directional taillights in all but the earliest; V. Winn comment. The 3600 trolley trailer has the same basic body as the 2036 but is unpowered; lacks a pantograph or current collector bow; has plastic 3000/1 wheels; sells for about 40 per cent of the powered unit; two seated figures in both passenger compartments; both discontinued in 1984; length 350 mm.
(A) 1978, red 2030/3 pantograph on roof of powered unit; yellow window frames; red supports on sides of body; no pin stripes on body. May not have been produced except as hand-made factory sample; R. Rench comment.
NRS
(B) 1978-84, 2036/3 current collector bow in place of pantograph; brown window frames; yellow pin stripes on body. **150**

Note: Two engines were given the same number, the 2040 steam locomotive and the 2040 electric.

2040: 1978-86, Ge 6/6 "Crocodile" locomotive of the Rhaetian Railway (RhB), the largest continuous metric gauge rail network in Europe encompassing almost 400 kilometers. Modeled after the largest standard locomotive series of the RhB, which was used as a heavy universal electric locomotive for goods and passenger traffic over mountain tracks. Although the photos in early catalogues depict the prototype, it is unlikely that a model of the prototype shown was produced. Three-piece articulated body, two motorized sections; length 560 mm; with 2030/3 pantographs, a dull

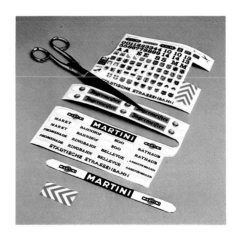

Both old-timer and contemporary streetcars and their trailers, 2035, 3500 and 2036, 3600, have always been packaged with peel-and-stick alternative signs and numbers.

Lehmann introduced its huge 2040 model of the Rhaetian Railway "crocodile" proclaiming its more than 600 parts. As in the prototype, both hoods are articulated to the main body suspended between them, enabling the locomotive to move through tight curves and esses with sinuous ease. A conspicuous variation since its introduction in 1978 has been the color of the roof insulators.

brown-finished body and several differences in the side vent and window detail. The following variations are known to exist:
(A) 1978, uncatalogued; has glossy, medium brown finish with light gray roof; silver, unpainted (bare metal) pantographs with only a single contact bar at top (early version of 2040/3); brown roof insulators; all-gray wheels which drive slanted drive rods; black grab-irons on main cab; translucent windows on main body (not windows to engineer's cabins) not blocked out with white color; light gray catwalks at edges of roof.   **1,200**
(B) 1978-79, same as (A), but wheels that drive slanted drive rods have black-painted centers.   **1,200**
(C) 1979-80, similar to (B), but with green roof insulators.   **675**
(D) 1980-81, similar to (B), but with red roof insulators.   **600**
(E) 1980-81, uncatalogued; similar to (B), but with combination of red and green roof insulators.   **600**

(F) 1983, body has glossy, bright red finish; red roof insulators. R. Enners Collection. Only two have been reported by Lehmann as a pre-production test.   **NRS**
(G) 1981-84, silver-painted pantographs with two contact bars at top (late version of 2040/3); red roof insulators; windows on main body blocked out with white; dark gray catwalks at edge of roof.   **500**
(H) 1985, similar to (G), but with yellow grab-irons on main body; yellow detail markings in lower right-hand corner of main body.   **425**
(I) 1985-86, similar to (H) but body color is orange-brown; lower head lamps have gold bezel rings.   **CP**
(J) 1986, body painted dark green but otherwise similar to (I); only one made for pre-production test. R. Enners Collection.   **NRS**

2045: 1986, Ge 2/4 (1'B1') passenger locomotive of the RhB, with slanting drive rod, open driver's cab door with adjustable sliding windows; numbered 205, shown in 1983-84 catalogue with two silver 2040/3 pantographs; red roof insulators; body is same orange-brown color as 2040(I) crocodile. The 1983-84 catalogue depicts this locomotive with solid guide wheels; however the 1985-86 catalogue version is shown with spoked guide wheels. This later version is apparently the only one produced.
(A) 1986, dark green-painted body, pre-production prototype. R. Enners Collection.   **NRS**
(B) 1986, brown-painted body as seen in 1985 and 1986-87 catalogues. The first production run of this locomotive has Eberhard Richter's signed initials on opposing side cab doors, a gesture to memorialize his spirit and work in bringing about LGB; W. Richter comment. Eberhard Richter died December 30, 1984 (see "Despeche" magazine, Spring 1985). 2000 of these locomotives were produced; models produced afterward will not bear Mr. Richter's initials.   **400**

2046: 1986, a red 300 mm long rack locomotive with a silver roof built as Zahnrad-Ellok HGe 2/2 for the Furka-Oberalpbahn; has 2040/3 pantograph and three lamps at each end; markings include "FO", "21", "HGe 2/2", "25t" and silver manufacturer's plaque on each side. This locomotive is capable of pulling 25 percent grades.   **CP**

Electrification of parts of the present Rhaetan Railway, in southeastern Switzerland, occurred in the 1920s. Continuing their series of cars and locomotives from this largest European narrow gauge network, Lehmann introduced in 1986 this old-style boxcab electric with its slanting jackshaft drive.

Chapter IV
Diesel Locomotives and Railbuses

Diesel locomotives bear a German name, and it is not surprising that Lehmann has found attractive prototypes, both large and small. Although American diesels are almost all diesel-electrics, with the diesel engines driving generators which power motors on each engine axle, Lehmann identifies its prototypes as diesel-hydraulics, in which the diesel engine operates a pump or impeller to drive oil against a turbine connected to the axles.

209: 1975-86, Kof diesel-hydraulic shunter and main line locomotive with side rods. Battery-powered model similar to 2090, but with medium green body; red plastic drive wheels. **CP**

2051: 1979-86, V51/V52 series B'B' (Bo Bo class) twin-diesel locomotive, modeled after one of the five modern diesel-hydraulic bogie locomotives acquired by the German Federal Railways (DB) in the early 1960s for their narrow gauge lines in Wurttemberg. A white stripe may be found in complete or incomplete configurations (on recent models) or may be altogether absent (on older versions) around the edges of the catwalks on the chassis; length 436 mm.

(A) 1979, dull red finish; red grab-irons, "252 901-4" on sides of cab and over radiator grills front and rear; large "DB" logo; early 2030/1 red wheels; hood steps quite pronounced; white horizontal stripe along sides of body; white stripe on chassis only along lateral catwalks; may be the prototype. **NRS**

(B) 1979, similar to (A), but with dull brick red finish; black grab-irons; numbered "251902-3", a smaller "DB" logo; metal manufacturer's plaque added to lower center of each side of front hood; white stripe on body, but none on chassis; has red 2030/1 wheels. **450**

(C) 1980, same as (B), but with 2035/1 black wheels. **425**

(D) 1981-86, similar to (C), but with shiny, lighter red finish; white stripe on chassis is usually complete around all edges of catwalks, has dimension markings at chassis ends. **CP**

2051S: 1981-86, same as 2051(C) or (D); earliest models may have also been produced in a red color similar to 2051(A). These models have electronic diesel and horn sounds. **CP**

The massive 2051S has a throaty diesel roar that idles at low throttle, a mechanically triggered horn and the EAV electronically delayed start. Five prototypes were placed in service in Baden-Wurttemberg in 1964, and all are still in use, on other lines. Lehmann rates this its most powerful diesel model, able to haul 52 axles.

2060: 1969-82, Schoma CFL-150 DH (B-class) industrial diesel locomotive for main line service and shunting; red body on gray or black chassis; mock roof horn may be black or dull or shiny "gold"-finished; hazard markings are red and white or yellow and black; length 270 mm.

(A) 1969-70, red, rather dull finished, unpainted body; may be faded or pinkish-red on some pieces; without embossed manufacturer's plaques or numbers; roof horn usually black. May have been the prototype. **NRS**

(B) 1970-74, same as (A), but with embossed manufacturer's plaque; white-painted "60" on cab; red and white hazard markers at each corner of chassis. **145**

(C) 1974-76, same as (A), but with gold finish on embossed manufacturer's plaque; white-painted "60" on cab; red and white hazard markers at each corner of chassis. **145**

(D) 1975-82, shiny painted red finish; embossed manufacturer's plaques; white-painted "60" on cab; red and white hazard markers at each corner of chassis; roof horn usually black. Has lighting socket. **125**

(E) 1978, similar to (D), but body painted royal blue; embossed markings not distinguished with gold or paint; gray chassis; made for Primus. H. Banzaf Collection. **NRS**

The horn was added to the yellow 2060 in 1971, a year after the model was catalogued in three colors (yellow, 2060Y; red, 2060 and green, 2060G). 2060H now has a battery recharged by track current to maintain a steady volume of blare regardless of speed.

The latest in the 2060 series, 2061 wears the livery of the Furka-Oberalp, part of the Swiss Rhaetian network. It has been used in several special uncatalogued sets.

(F) 1982, same as (D), but with gold finish on embossed manufacturer's plaques. **125**

2060G: 1970-75, same basic locomotive as the 2060, but with unpainted medium green body with black grab-irons; red chassis, black horn; white embossed "60" and gold-finished manufacturer's plaque on cab; clear windows and engineer in cab. No lighting socket.
(A) Red chassis. **225**
(B) Black chassis. **250**

2060H: 1971-86, same basic locomotive as the 2060, but with semi-glossy unpainted yellow body; red and white hazard markers on front and back ends; an electric horn concealed under the body; black air tanks, grab-irons, light covers at each end; black horn on gray roof; gold rim on cab and door window panels; gold raised panel with "SCHOEMA" and more information in two panels; length 270 mm.
(A) 1971-72, horn mechanism inside cab, concealed by opaque, black windows; roof is screwed on with screw-heads showing at each corner; white "60"; window frames and embossed gold-finished manufacturer's plaque; no 2110 contact shoes; black chassis. **NRS**
(B) 1973-74, same as (A), but with 2110 contact shoes present; red chassis. **150**
(C) 1975-79, horn mechanism inside of front motor hood; cab windows clear; engineer figure inside cab; red chassis. **150**
(D) 1980-85, same as (C), but with rechargeable battery for horn mechanism. **CP**
(E) 1985, yellow portion of body is painted bright glossy yellow with black stripes on hoods (of the same design as the 2061); hood vents and other embossed markings are painted black. A black-painted "2060" on cab just below manufacturer's plaque replaces the embossed "60" of the other versions (no gold plating on plaque); other black-painted cab markings include: "Gew. Lok 22t/P 18t", "Br. Gew./G 15t", "Vmax 30km/h" and "Br. Unt. 1.3.84 Nur"; chassis is painted bright red with white dimension markings on each end; black tanks on each side of chassis have the markings: "Kraftstoff 3601". **CP**

2060P: 1984, same basic locomotive as the 2060, but with dark blue-painted body with same two horizontal white stripes on both sides of hood and grill similar to the 2061; white "PHILIPS LOK 1" markings on cab; red chassis with yellow grab-irons; black air tanks and step protrusions on side of chassis. Windows have yellow frames, black shading on charcoal gray roof; gold-colored whistle on roof, black-colored head and taillights at each end of cab; sold only with set 380.7080 (also known as 20517). Price for set: **250**

2060Y: 1970-78, same basic locomotive as the 2060H(A) or (B), but without the electric horn mechanism. **150**
(A) 1970-72, similar externally to 2060H(A); black chassis. **135**
(B) 1972-74, similar to (A), but without gold finish on embossed manufacturer's plaque; clear windows; red or gray chassis. **135**
(C) 1976-78, similar to (A), but without gold finish on embossed manufacturer's plaque; clear windows; "LGB Junior" embossed on underside of chassis. Originally sold with "Junior" set 20501L. **NRS**

2061: 1983-86, Swiss diesel shunter or light line locomotive of the Furka-Oberalp line (part of the Rhaetian system). Same basic body configuration as the 2060(C); shiny red-painted body with white horizontal stripes on both hoods and white radiator grills; some may have "2060" on the underside of chassis rather than the correct "2061"; came with engineer.
(A) 1983, light gray chassis with black grab-irons; white "Furka-Oberalp" over "2061" above "Tm 2/2 SCHLEPP VMAX 45KM T218t" all on cab side adjacent to door; lower vent screens (two per side on lower sides of forward hood) are painted black or gray to simulate wire mesh. **160**
(B) 1983, uncatalogued; same as (A), but with yellow grab-irons; came with or without "FO" on cab doors; may have black (B. Roth comment) or dark gray chassis; issued with set 20401RZ as well as separately. **160**
(C) 1983, same as (B), but hood screens are red rather than black or gray; C. Colwell comment. **NRS**
(D) 1983-86, same as (A), but with yellow grab-irons; black or medium gray chassis (B. Roth comment); issued with set 20512 and separately; black chassis is the only catalogued version. **CP**
(E) 1984, uncatalogued; deep red-painted body, darker than in the above pieces; dark gray chassis, same as 2060; yellow grab-irons; without "2061", "Furka-Oberalp" and other previously described cab markings which are replaced by "Gew. Lok: 22t" over "Br.Gew. P 18t/G 15t" over "Vmax 30km/h" over "Br. Unt. 1.3. 84 AW Nur"; lower vent screens same color as body; sold only with set 20401RZ. **NSS**
(F) 1984, uncatalogued; same as (D), but with "Furka-Oberalp" across lower portion of cab doors; sold only with set 20401RZ. **NSS**

2064 1986, a red railcar with a silver roof and green and white horizontal stripes around body just beneath windows; this car is essentially the same as a single unit of the 2065 which it now replaces; black-painted flying locomotive wheel on side of body. Production model will have special lighting and sound. **CP**

2065: 1981-85, Wismar twin-unit railbus "Triebwagen" (also inappropriately dubbed "Galloping Goose") modeled after a second class internal combustion engined railcar. Maximum economy was achieved by equipping passenger coaches with their own drive systems, especially since goods wagons could also be hauled; has two powered units each capable of independent travel; 2206 motor mounted beneath floor. When used together and joined with wiring junction lead, the head and taillights automatically change with direction. Cars were produced with exact details depicted in the 1981-82, 1983-84 and 1985-86 catalogues. Discontinued in 1985. The most recent models come with seated driver and standing hostess; interior lighting; EAV system; 2065/3 decal sheet. **425**

2066: 1981-86, Wismar Hannover E "Anteater" railbus of the German Railway Association; model T41-DEV with red and white body, black chassis; automatically reversing head and taillights, interior lighting; comes with seated driver, standing hostess; luggage rack kit; 2065/3 decal sheet. Although the photograph of the prototype depicts red radiators, detailed head lamps and silver handrails, the most recent production models come detailed exactly as depicted in the 1981-82, 1983-84 and 1985-86 catalogues; length 445 mm. **CP**

Although now available as a single unit, 2065 originally was marketed only in pairs. Some American sellers have misnamed these flat-fronted railcars "Galloping Goose," after a famous long-snouted Western railcar. As with the streetcars, the motorman (and, here, ticket taker) have magnetized bases and can be moved when direction is reversed; the lights reverse auomatically, as on most recent Lehmann locomotives.

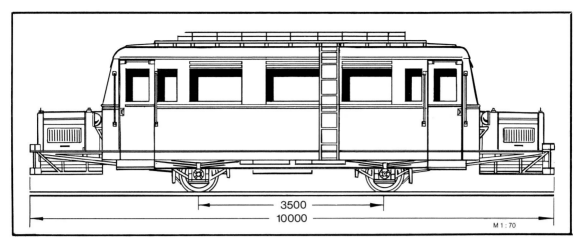

If any of the Lehmann railbuses deserves the American soubriquet "Galloping Goose," 2066 is it; but the Germans called these double-ended red and white vehicles "anteater" or "pig's-snout" for their conspicuously protruding motor hoods with baggage racks.

2090: 1977-85, "Kof" diesel-hydraulic shunter and main line locomotive with side rods; similar to locomotives in service on many municipal railways and the North-German Island railway, the Nassau narrow gauge railway and the Zillertal railway. Has non-working head and taillights; length 240 mm. This locomotive was produced in both green and red; the green version appears to be very rare. Not all 2090s had black running boards as found on later 2090Ns; B. Roth comment.
(A) 1977-78, unpainted green body; red chassis; smooth light gray roof without any details or rain gutters; windshields lack wiper blades; cab has a black "LGB" plaque with white heat-stamped lettering above a smaller black plaque with white "2065"; green grab-irons and head lamp bezels, but no light bulbs; no engineer in cab; has early "disc-type" drive wheels. **NRS**

(B) 1977-78, same as (A), but with black grab-irons. **NRS**
(C) 1979-80, similar to (A), but with unpainted red body which may be faded or pinkish-red on some pieces; running boards have gaps and lack "diamond-plate" appearance; gaps in running boards as well as side air tank for use on battery model as well; black bell and black air vent on roof; black grab-irons. **100**
(D) 1980-81, red body same as (C); gray chassis; roof with distinct rain gutters at lateral edges, simulated hatches on top and bell; same plaque placement on cab as (A), but upper plaque has "D10" in white figures, the small lower plaque has white "2090"; black grab-irons and head lamp bezels; white detail markings on cab doors; engineer inside cab. **90**
(E) 1982-85, same as (D), but with red-painted body. **85**
2090N: 1983-86, similar to 2090(D), but with yellow body; black chassis;

Obviously aimed at the lower end of the price market, 2090N's three headlights are not operating. Its yellow body replaces a common red and a rarer green predecessor.

2096S differs from 2095 in its two-tone livery, which matches passenger car 3064, rather than the solid red of 2095 and 3063. And, of course, 2096S has a sound system (motor roar and two-tone horn). The European designation of the two-wheeled power trucks with zero idler wheels is "Bo-Bo," by which easily pronounceable name the locomotive is known to many Americans.

black or white detail markings on cab doors. "Lok Gew 18 Ot" and "Br. Gew 14 5t". Referred to in 1986-87 catalogue only as 2090. **CP**

2095: 1973-85, B'B' (Bo Bo class) twin-diesel bogie locomotive of the Austrian Federal Railways series 2095.11; has drive rods with exterior counter weights known as Hal cranks; forward and rear heralds embossed and painted silver as are the numbers, numbers on sides of body are similar; red-painted body; gray chassis; length 460 mm.

(A) 1973-78, small pinkish-red plaque with white markings next to cabin doors glued into small depression in body; silver-painted horizontal body molding, actually a composite of three parallel moldings running around the middle of body; only white markings on medium gray chassis consist of fill-level numbers on fuel tank; early 2030/1 red wheels. See LGB Depesche 19/20 1973; piece not catalogued until 1974. Early 2095s did not have a lighting socket; B. Roth comment. **350**

(B) 1979-80, same as (A), but with four additional white detail markings at intervals along sides of chassis just below seam of body and chassis. **300**

(C) 1981-82, same as (A), but with small plaque next to doors molded with body; four additional white detail markings at intervals along sides of chassis just below seam of body and chassis. **250**

(D) 1981-82, uncatalogued; same as (C), but with horizontal mid-body molding painted black. **325**

(E) 1983-84, same as (C), but with black 2035/1 wheels. **250**

(F) 1984-85, same as (E), with lighter gray-painted chassis. **250**

2095N: 1986, similar to 2095(F) but lacks embossed heralds and has modern OBB paint scheme; red paint is darker than in the 2095(F) dark chassis and white markings reflect changes in OBB logo design: OBB on side is smaller, under white builders' plaque with red letters (rather than red with white letters), and bold white logo resembling an S replaces winged wheel logo on front; logo also at side rear. **CP**

2096S: 1983-86, B'B' bogie locomotive, OBB series 2095 in authentic beige and red; other technical data are the same as the 2095(F) locomotive; comes with an EAV system; two-tone horn and diesel engine sounds in a package containing one 2060/3 contact strip to activate horn; black 2035/1 wheels. Aside from its colors the basic external differences between the 2096S and the 2095 are that later versions of the 2096s have a decal instead of the embossed road name logo on front and rear ends of body and all versions have a beige brake hose on the driver's side of body rather than a black one at both ends. However, the embossed logo on the earlier 2096S may be prototypical and not put into regular production (confirmation requested). Manufacturer's plaque changed from molded-on plastic to brass, etched and glued to side of body; R. Rench comment.

(A) 1983, embossed road name heralds on front and rear ends beneath windshields; may be prototype model only. **NRS**

(B) 1983-86, road name logos on front and rear ends beneath windshields are in the form of decals, not embossed. **CP**

Chapter V
Rolling Stock Descriptions

Interchangeability of parts marks many series, particularly the 300 mm cars, both freight and passenger. These standard parts have their own history, independent of and broader in scope than the histories of individual cars. Often, as with changes in couplers, railings and wheels, they serve to date an individual car within a long production period.

300 mm CHASSIS FRAME MARKINGS

The earlier four-wheel coaches and freight cars lacked "painted-on" chassis frame markings. The 1979-1980 and 1982-1983 catalogues depicted most four-axle cars in the 300 mm series with the following Type 1 frame markings:

Gew. 5650kg   LuP 6,74m   Rev. 10. 77

These markings were altered slightly in 1983 as indicated in the 1983-1984 catalogue, and appeared as the Type 2 markings:

Gew. 5650kg   LuP 6,75 | Rev | 3. | 7. | 87 |

Chassis frame markings were changed again in about mid-1984 and at the time of this writing have not been catalogued; these are the Type 3 markings:

←(-)→   Lup 6,75   3,1m   Gew.5650kg | Rev | 3. | 7. | 87 |

Although these frames have always been manufactured in black plastic the company began to paint the frames in flat black from time to time beginning in 1980. This was most prevalent in anniversary cars and limited production items. In 1984 all rolling stock began routinely to appear with flat black painted frames.

ROOF TYPES

There are five basic roof styles used on the LGB coaches and boxcars: Medium-Arched, Clerestory, Tapered-Arched, Low-Arched and High-Arched.

The earliest versions of all these roofs were unpainted light gray. Around 1976 the company began to add shading to the edges of the roof in the form of a swatch of flat black paint giving them a weathered appearance. The next change took place about 1979 with the roofs being painted light, glossy gray with the black edge shading. This color is most common on the larger eight-wheel coaches, the 3060, 3061, 3063 and 3064. In 1982 a medium greenish-gray color with black edge shading was used on most car roofs. This version is currently used today; however, in mid-1984 the company changed the roof molds, adding a textured appearance to many of the roof styles.

Medium-Arched: this roof has been produced in seven basic types. It has a Medium-Arch which appears to have three centers of radius forming the curvature of the roof .

MA1. For 300 mm long cars, completely smooth and lacks seams or bands across top; used on 3007, 3008, 3009, 3019 and 3019N, and 4029 prior to 1971.

MA2. Similar to MA1, but with six seams or bands across top; used on later versions of same cars as well as the 3007LJ and 3013LJ.

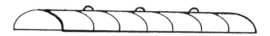

MA3. Similar to MA2, but with three very small simulated vents equally spaced; used on 1982, 1983, 1984, 3007BZ, 3007MF and 3007PB, and 3019 beginning in 1982

MA4. For 460 mm long cars, seven seams or bands across top; used on 3063 and 3064 coaches prior to 1979 and on the 3062.

MA5. Similar to MA4, but with three black roof vents; used on 3063 and 3064 coaches beginning about 1979.

MA6. For 550 mm long cars, ten seams or bands running lengthwise along top and three small vents; used on 3067 beginning in 1986.

MA7. Similar to MA6, but with one large vent added over center of dining area; used on 3068 beginning in 1986.

Clerestory: this roof has been produced in four basic versions, with a raised construction atop the roof with windows and/or vents for admitting light and air.

CL1. For 300 mm long cars, roof with short Clerestory that stops about 25 mm from each end of the roof; used on 3010, 3011 and 3012. The Clerestory itself has six small yellow windows and five covered vents on each side. Also called a deck roof; R. Rench comment.

CL2. For 300 mm long cars, flat roof with full Clerestory that extends to the ends of the roof; the Clerestory itself has eight small yellow windows on each side and four vents atop Clerestory; used on 3050 coach.

CL3. Same basic design as CL1, but for 420 mm long coaches. Low-Arched roof has stove stacks; Clerestory itself has eight small window frames on each side and no obvious vents; used on 3060 and 3061 coaches.

CL4. For 495 mm long cars, Low-Arched roof with the Clerestory rounded downward at the ends, 12 small windows on each side and stove stacks at opposite corners; used on 3080 and 3081 coaches. These roofs were painted silver in production units; black shading was added to the edges of later versions and the most recent variation is dark greenish-gray with black edge shading. This roof is know to have had a slight texturing on all variations with the exception of the prototypes. Also called a railroad roof; R. Rench comment.

Low-Arched: this roof has been produced in four styles and may have a slight rounded arch or two flat pieces with a low-centered ridge.

LA1. This roof is for 300 mm long cars, arched slightly from edge to edge, has six seams across the top and has two roof vents, one each between the second and third and the fourth and fifth seams, used on 3000, 3006, 3013, 3014, 3015, 4030, 4031, 4032, 4032L and 4033.

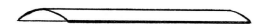

LA2. Similar to LA1, but without seams and vents; surface is lightly textured, used on 4035.

LA3. For a 430 mm long boxcar, this version has 10 seams across the top and two rails on each side to fit atop sliding doors; used on 4063 boxcar.

LA4. For 415 mm long cars, this version is not curved but is composed of two flat, pitched portions that peak at the center like a conventional house roof. There is a catwalk down the center and 12 seams across the top; used on 4064, 4067, 4070 and 4071.

Tapered-Arched: this roof has been produced in three versions and used on only two cars.

TA1. For 300 mm cars a flattened 300 mm roof which is slightly rounded and tapered toward edges and ends; top is completely smooth, without seams; used on 3040 coach until about 1974.

TA2. Similar to TA1, but with seven seams or bands across top; used on 3040 coach beginning about 1975.

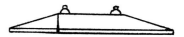

TA3. The basic design is similar to other Tapered-Arched roofs but is very short (for 170 mm long cars) with two small, simulated roof vents; used on 3041 excursion car.

High-Arched: this roof has been catalogued in two versions and has a single High-Arch.

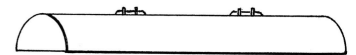

HA1. This roof is rather strongly arched, for 495 mm long cars and has two vents that are molded with the roof itself; used on 3070 and 3071.

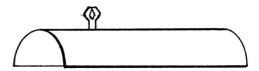

HA2. Only about two-thirds as long as the HA1 version, it lacks vents but has a smokestack, and was to be used on 4075 service wagon, which has not yet gone into production.

COUPLERS, TALGOS & SIDE FRAMES

Plastic wheels, a narrow coupling loop and the thick, untapered hook mark this as an early locomotive.

Couplers

There are four basic versions of the standard coupler hooking arms. The earliest three versions, from about 1969 to about 1980, have a distinctly triangular-shaped hook and a coiled metal return spring. The first of these is distinguished from the

Hooks were riveted in place up to the mid-1970s, as on this 4040 ET tank car.

second by its uncoupling pad at the inner end of the hook arm: thick, with a round almost semi-cylindrical bottom when seen in profile, and a horizontal top. After 1972 and by 1974, probably that is sometime during 1973, the uncoupling pad profile had changed: the top now raked downward from the hook toward the center of the car at about a 40 degree angle, resulting in a thinner total pad. In the mid to late 1970s, definitely before 1979 and perhaps as early as 1977, a change was made in the method of hook attachment, which distinguished the first two versions from the third.

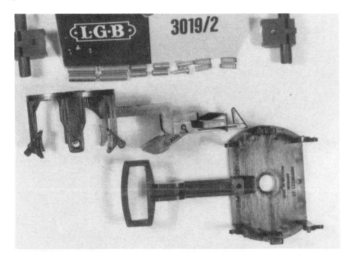

This intermediate coupler, still with the old triangular hook, has a newer peg pressed into a keyhole slot replacing the rivet of the older style.

Early versions (from the beginning) were attached with a horizontal rivet which was inserted then heated to permanently secure it. If a hook was broken, the rivet would have to be cut off and a new one used to re-attach a new hook. Therefore, a new type of hook and keyhole mount was designed which was faster to assemble and cheaper to manufacture.

The pre-1981 coupler hook has a large pad, and its metal coiled spring is hidden. Plastic axles were introduced in 1978.

The hook of this third early version has "ears". They extend from each side of its shank and they snapped into keyhole-shaped openings on the talgos. These variations can be significant in determining the vintage of some cars.

The more recent variety, from 1979-1980 on, has a less angular-shaped hook which is slightly rounded and has a small "barb" on the inside portion of the hook for more secure coupling. The uncoupler pad is quite thin, and curved rather like a comma in profile.

A post-1980 coupler, with its serpentine flat plastic "bed-spring," called by upholsterers a "no-sag spring," is clearly visible on either side of the hook's narrow uncoupling pad. Notice the marked taper on the hook. These features facilitate depolarized coupling when hooks are installed at both ends of a car, allowing easy mating and sprung lateral motion. The screw holding the wide coupling loop to the talgo is a late feature, allowing home installation of a second hook.

The spring is different as well, being a flat plastic "bedspring"-style which allows better flexibility and sideways action of the coupler arm. The pivot of the hook arms on the early version is a single plastic rivet which passes horizontally through the arm, permitting only vertical arm movements. From 1979-1980 a plastic rivet passes vertically through the arm, allowing increased side to side movements. The newer loops are wider and have beveled edges, greatly improving coupling on curves. Note: all of 1985 shipments are being packed with an extra coupler hook; G. Nicholson comment.

The wide coupling loop and the slender, markedly tapered hook are late features.

Talgos

The talgos, like the hooking arms, were produced in two basic versions. The earliest of these was produced with the coupler assembly (hooking loop and hooking arm support) molded with the talgo as a single unit. This loop on the hook end has a wider contact surface with a notch to maintain alignment of the hooking arm. The newer versions have the

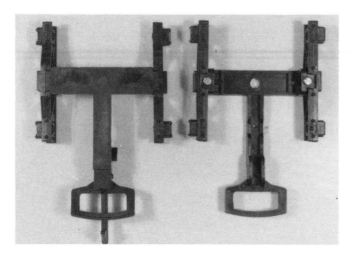

Early talgo trucks have narrow coupling loops permanently attached.

talgo and coupler pieces cast separately with the hooking loops attached with a screw. This change allowed the hooking arms to be attached to either talgo, providing a means for bi-directional coupling and uncoupling.

Side Frames

The side frames used on most rolling stock pieces were cast in black plastic. In about mid-1983 many side frames were cast in a slate gray plastic. This characteristic change is most common in the arch bar-style side frames used on the United States prototype four-axle cars and the 4062, 4063 and 4069 European versions. Late 1985 production shows return to black side frames. Trucks (bogies) are of four types, according to the method of springing.

3000/3: leaf springs above the journal boxes, used on passenger cars 3060 through 3064.
3080/2: a combination of transverse leaf springs between coil

The four types of truck or bogie, from top to bottom: 3000/3, used on 3060-64; 3080/2, used on 3080-81; 3070/2, used on 3070-71 and 4000/2, used on all freight cars with trucks.

springs; "Commonwealth" trucks, used on 3080 and 3081.
3070/2: leaf springs beneath journal boxes, used on 3070 and 3071.
4000/2: coil springs; arch bar trucks, used on all four-axle freight cars.

WHEEL TYPES

The distinctive heavy metal axle was used on pre-1978 passenger cars.

The early wheels (Type E1, spoked 3000/1 or solid 4000/1) have slightly thicker rims and taller flanges than more recently produced wheels. The most distinguishing character of the early wheel sets is the shiny, exposed metal axle which is notably thicker than the later axles. The early wheels were cast separately and slipped onto each end of the one-piece stud axle and are not removable from axle. Type E2 wheels (spoked or solid) have the same basic shapes and dimensions as the E1 wheels but do not have the thick metal axle exposed between the wheels. The metal axle itself is a slender shaft concealed except at the ends by the hollow axle portions cast as part of the wheels. Early battery-operated sets did not have a metal axle concealed within the plastic; B. Roth comment.

Since 1978, wheels have been mounted on metal axle cores concealed in plastic, which reduces rusting from outdoor use.

The Type L wheels (spoked or solid) are very similar to E2 but have shorter flanges. Perhaps the most notable difference between E and L wheels is that during operation the former types will cause the cars to bounce when riding over switches or crossings since the flanges are too tall to clear the frogs!

The E1 wheels were used on rolling stock dating from 1969 to about 1978. E2 wheels first appeared in 1978 and were replaced by L wheels beginning in 1979. L wheels are used on currently produced pieces.

BODY TYPES

Variations in body types for 3000 Series 300 mm coaches, 3000, 3006, 3007, 3008, 3009, 3010, 3011, 3012, 3013, 3014, 3015 and 3040, are based mainly on materials represented (either Simulated Wood or Simulated Metal), number of windows, end door arrangement, narrow or squarish window shape and the presence of vertical and/or horizontal seams. End doors on all these cars open out, but only since about 1981 have they had operating latches. Longer four-axle coach body types are also described here.

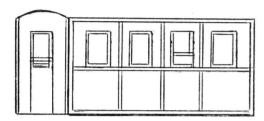

SM1. Simulated Metal body with four narrow windows and centered end doors; five vertical seams (including corners), three horizontal seams—one just below window bases and at upper and lower edges of the body; raised number-boards, used for 3007 (1971-1972), 3008, 3009 (1971-1973), 3010 (1969-1980), 3011 (1971-1978) and 3012 (1971-1978).

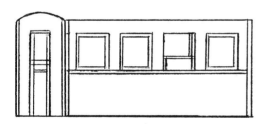

SM2. Simulated Metal body with four squarish windows and centered end doors; corner seams and a single horizontal seam level with window bases
(A) This car has raised number-boards and logo plaques when used for 3007 series (1974-1982), 3008 (1973-1978) and 3013 (1973-1980).
(B) The sides are smooth without raised number-boards and logo plaques when used for 1982, 1983, 1984, 3007 series (1983-1986), 3007LJ (1981), 3013 (1981-1985) and 3013LJ (1981).

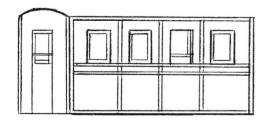

SM3. Simulated Metal body with five vertical seams (including corners) and four horizontal seams, two of the latter are closely aligned and just below the bases of the narrow windows; raised

number-boards and logo plaques; used for 3010 (1981-1985), 3011 (1979-1985), 3012 (1979-1986), 3014 (1979-1982) and 3015 (1979-1986).

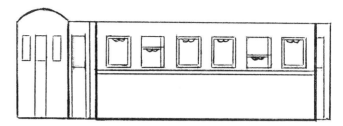

SM4. For 460 mm coaches, Simulated Metal body with six windows and two recessed outside doors on each side, two small windows and centered door on each end; used for 3062, 3063 and 3064.
(A) The door hinge pinions and the pinion holes on the body are small, having a diameter of about 1-1/2 mm. The rectangular recesses at the lower left-hand corner on sides of body if exposed by missing number-board are relatively deep, about 1 mm. If they are not exposed there is a small, plastic rectangular number-board within the depression; used for 3062 (1976-1980), 3063 (1975-1980) and 3064 (1977-1980).
(B) Same as (A), but rectangular depressions (same position as A) are only superficially expressed, much less than 1 mm. Small plastic rectangular number-boards not used; used on 3062 (1981-1986).
(C) The door hinge pinions and the pinion holes on the body are relatively large, having a diameter of more than 2 mm. The rectangular recesses in lower left-hand corner of body are the same as (B); used in 3063 (1981-86) and 3064 (1981-86).
SM5. For 495 mm European coaches. Simulated Metal body with broad operating windows and centered end doors. Used on 3070 and 3071.
(A) Six windows; 3070.
(B) Three windows, a pair of hinged bi-fold operating baggage compartment doors with two very narrow windows, and a fourth broad window; 3071.

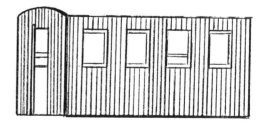

SW1. Simulated Wood; paneled slat-sided body with vertical seams, slightly raised number-boards and logo plaque (if present) on sides, four narrow windows on each side and centered end doors; used for 3000 and 3006 series cars.

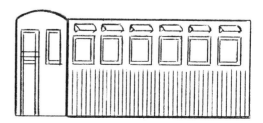

SW2. Similar to SW1, but with six windows on each side and one window and an offset door on ends; used only for 3040.

(A) Tall window openings to accommodate taller window frames, each having a large louvered vent at the top molded with the frame itself to form a single unit, used for 3040 coaches from 1969 to 1978.

(B) Short window openings with a louvered vent molded over each window opening as a part of the body; used for 3040 coaches from 1979 to 1986.

SW3. For 495 mm American coaches. Simulated Wood; paneled slat-sided body with narrow, vertical windows and centered end doors. Used on 3080 and 3081.

(A) Nine windows; 3080.

(B) Five windows, baggage compartment door, and a sixth window; 3081.

CHASSIS TYPES FOR 300 mm ROLLING STOCK

There are basically three versions of chassis frames used on all two-axle, 300 mm long cars. Of these versions there are also early (1968-1970) and late (1971-1986) variations. The early variety lacks the two square-shaped screw receptacles (for mounting 5005 track cleaners) on the cross members adjacent to and between the pivoting truck assemblies. Early frames also lack holes for the truss rods attached to many of the freight cars. Later versions have both of these features.

Single brakeman platform chassis: this version has two horizontal slots (aproximately 10 mm long x 1 mm high) at only one end of chassis to take the securing tabs for the brakeman platform pieces. This chassis has been used on 3019, 3019N, 3020, 4029, 4030, 4031 series, 4032 series, 4033 and 4034.

Dual brakeman platform chassis: this version has two horizontal slots (approximately 10 mm long x 1 mm high) at each end of chassis to take the securing tabs for the brakeman platform pieces. The chassis was used on 3000, 3006 series, 3007 series (includes applicable anniversary cars), 3008, 3009, 3010, 3011, 3012, 3013, 3014, 3015, 3040, 3050, all 4040 tankers with LT tanks, 4041 and 4041G and on 4042 produced after 1982.

Full load capacity chassis: this version completely lacks the above described slots. This chassis has been used on 4000, 4001, 4002, 4003 series, 4010, 4011 (both models), 4020, 4021, 4035, 4036, 4040 tankers with ET tanks, 4042 (prior to 1982) and may have been used on the 3050.

Although these chassis applications follow a production purpose some different combinations may appear due to shortages at the factory or alterations by consumers. For example, 4010 gondolas could easily take any of the chassis types but a 3015 coach can only have the dual brakeman platform chassis with some modification.

RAILINGS

Platforms (for brakemen) are common on European freight cars as well, of course, as on the early passenger cars, without vestibules, commonly found on narrow gauge lines. A very high percentage of LGB rolling stock thus comes with railed platforms. They differ primarily in solidity (solid wall, solid wall with central aisleway, open frame) and attached fixtures (type of side gate, accordion central gate, relief or separately cast brake hoses and brakewheel shafts).

There are two basic types: solid sheet metal wall, eventually replaced with solid wall with accordion-gated (or otherwise closed) central aisleway; and open frame, usually made of angle iron, occasionally of rods.

Type S. 1968-1985, solid, includes SW (Solid Wall) and SA (Solid wall with aisleway, usually Accordion-gated).

The SW1 railing, used on freight cars until 1978, has a Solid Wall with triangular gates. A. Rudman Collection.

SW1. 1968-1978, Solid Wall, for freight and postal cars. Simulated metal wall, rounded at corners; two tapered vertical braces cast into exterior of wall; triangular side gates, the slanting member running up toward the car; freestanding brakewheel shaft, with crank handle, attached outside at left of usually the loop end of the car; two low-relief brake pipes, the right one with low-relief hose, cast on outside of wall. Used on 4029, 4030, 4031, 3019 and 3020.

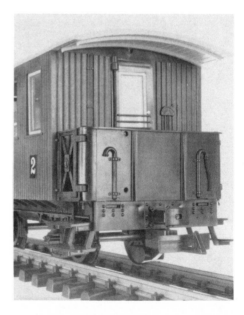

Old passenger cars have this Solid Wall SW2 railing, with rectangular side gates. Both this solid railing and its Accordion-gated successor are prototypical. A. Rudman collection.

SW2. 1968-1978, Solid Wall, for passenger cars. Similar to SW1, but has rectangular side gates, with "X" struts and a small boss where the struts intersect. Used on 3000, 3008, 3009, 3010, 3011 and 3012.

SW3. 1974-1985. Solid Wall, for larger old passenger cars. Similar to SW1, but no tapered braces; brakewheel shaft is cast in relief, with separate lever handle; and solid side gates. Used on 3060, 3061.

Three variations on 4031 have freight railings from different periods. Left is the FA4 Frame of Angle iron, with its vertical tread plate, stiff plastic chain and no side gates, beginning in 1981; center Solid rail SA1, with Accordion gated aisleway and triangular gates, 1979-80 and right, the old-style Solid Wall SW1 railing, with triangular side gates. C. Colwell Collection.

SA1. 1979-1980. Solid wall with Accordion-gate, for freight and postal cars. Similar to SW1, but with central portion of wall removed for access between cars, with an Accordion-gate attached to the exterior across the opening. Used only on these years' models of 4030, 4032 and 4033.

SA2. 1979-1985. Solid wall with Accordion-gate, for passenger cars. Similar to SW2, but the same modification as SA1 (central portion of wall removed for access between cars, with an Accordion-gate attached to the exterior across the opening). Differs from SA1 in having rectangular rather than triangular side gates. Used on later models of the same cars as SW2 and newer cars of similar type.

Type F. Open Frame, used on hoppers, late tank cars, recent freight and postal cars and American cars. Components are

Newer, short tank LT tankers have this Frame of Angle iron railing. The vertical tread plate is immovable on the model, but on the prototype lowers for access between cars.

simulated Angle iron (type FA) or simulated metal Rod (type FR).

FA. Frame made of simulated Angle iron.

FA1. Frame of Angle iron, used on 4041. Two horizontal and three vertical members, the middle one off-center to the left; the lower horizontal angle does not extend as far as the left vertical. Two brake pipes, the right one with hose attached. Grab-irons on outer vertical members. Two versions:
(A) Until circa 1979-1982, the brake pipes and hose are in the plane of the railing, and rather slender. Also used on 4041G.
(B) Since circa 1979-1982, the right-hand brake pipes and hoses, still vertical, are oriented at right angles to the plane of the railing, as a separate molding. Angle iron is slightly heavier than in (A).

FA2. 1979-1985. Frame of Angle iron, used on 4040 series tank cars with short tanks (type LT), at the platform end. Two narrow vertical rectangles of simulated Angle iron, joined by a raised immovable tread plate, each with one cross member. No chain across gap. Freestanding brake pipe and hose.

FA3. Frame of Angle iron, used on cars with brakeman's hut. A partial railing, with half freestanding and the other half cast in relief on the hut. Including the relief portion, consists of three vertical and two horizontal members. Brakewheel shaft cast in low relief on hut; housing for brakeshaft handle projects from wall. Grab-iron on each outer vertical. Used on 4062 and 4063. Two types:
(A) Up to circa 1979-1982, brake pipe and hose cast in low relief on hut wall.
(B) After circa 1979-1982, brake pipe and hose freestanding.

FA4. 1981-1985, for freight and postal cars. Somewhat similar to FA2, but wider, to match frame width; slightly thinner members; medial cross member is positioned higher; and chain across walkway joins the two sides. Unlike earlier freight railings, SW1 and SA1, FA4 has no side gates. Used on such cars as 4030, 3031, 4032, 4033, 4034 and 3019.

FR. Frame made of simulated metal Rods. Used on American cars.

FR1. Frame of Rods, used on 4065. Two inverted Us, joined by a chain. Brakeshaft and wheel in left part; roof ladder in right part at hook end (rear) of car.

FR2. Frame of Rods, used on 3080 and 3081. Two inverted Us, each with an additional vertical member, joined across the walkway by a chain, each with an outward bulge near the bottom of the outer vertical, as a grab-handle at the steps. Brakeshaft and wheel in the left half.

COLORS

Color differences are among the most immediately obvious variations. Since they often arise unintentionally, when a manufacturer provides a different shade of plastic or paint under the same number, and because Lehmann often continues prototype photos in the catalogue, many color variations within the same basic hue are uncatalogued. Naming them is often difficult; there have been, for example, several shades of what might be called "yellow" window frames on 300 mm passenger cars, which some describe as "orange," "beige," "light yellow," "bright yellow," "deep yellow," "yellow-orange," etc. If equipment acquired secondhand has an unusual color, it may be sun-faded; the black 4000 has shifted toward maroon, the green 3050 toward blue, after long exposure. It is important when making color comparisons to remember that adjacent colors and surface texture can distort psychological perception. This list both names colors and identifies some of the specific cars on which they are found.

REDS

There appear to be several variations of red plastic. However, they may all originally have been the same color when produced but fading may have caused some to turn a pinkish-red.
1. Semi-gloss pinkish-red: early 4065 and 2090.
2. Semi-gloss red: early 4040E and 4041.
There are five basic red paint shades.
1. Glossy red: 2095, most 3011, 3063 and 3064 .
2. Glossy cranberry: 2020LJ, some early 3011 and late 4041.
3. Dull dark red (almost brick red):   early 2051 and 4041 (circa 1980).
4. Glossy barn red (slightly more brown than glossy red): latest 3000.
5. Glossy boxcar brown-red: latest 4065.

GREENS

Green plastic variations are more difficult to describe.
1. Dull medium green (very similar to medium green paint): early 4068 and 2050.
2. Dull dark green (very similar to dark green paint):   early 4068 (probably second version), earliest 3019N.
3. Dull very dark green: some early 3010, earliest 3019, 3020, 2050 and 4047. Some early pieces appear to have a slightly bluish cast and may be a little darker than later pieces.
4. Dull medium-dark green: early 4011 and 4021.
5. Light green: earliest 3010.

At least two or perhaps three shades of green paint have been used. The most notable deviation from the usual green is on the 3060 coaches (circa 1977) whose paint is slightly lighter than a glossy dark green (medium-dark green).
1. Glossy medium green: latest 2050 and 3010.
2. Glossy dark green: 3070-71 and 3007MF.

BLUES

Blue plastic: flat medium blue as seen on the early blue steeple-cab locomotive 2031.

Blue paint: four shades of blue paint have been used, the darker ones more recently; listed in order of increasing darkness.
1. Glossy medium-light (or powder) blue: blue 4040A
2. Glossy medium blue: 3012, 3015, early 3013 and 2030.
3. Glossy royal blue: 20301BZ, later and the 3013.
4. Glossy dark blue (very slightly purplish):   1983, 1984, 1985 and the 20517 set.

ORANGES

Orange paint has not been used on production models; all pieces are in bright, unpainted orange plastic with a semi-gloss finish (i.e. late 4041, late 4011 and 2033).

YELLOWS

Yellow plastic appears in several versions.
1. Light lemon-yellow: used on earliest 3510 and the window frames on very early 300 mm coaches.
2. Flat, rich lemon-yellow: 2060H, 2035, 3500, 2090N and

3510 (circa 1979).
3. Orange-yellow used on window frames on most 300 mm coaches, beginning around 1971.
Lemon-yellow paint, the only yellow used, has only been used on the latest 2060H and perhaps the 20532 Schweiger set.

BROWNS

Brown plastic comes in four versions.
1. Straw brown (tan):   early 3007, 4010, 4020, 4029 and 4030.
2. Orange-brown: 4010, 4030, 4035, 4060, 4067 (SP and latest D.&R.G.).
3. Dark brown (somewhat darker, perhaps less red, than #4 painted):   early 3000, 2010 and the ties of most track.
4. Very dark brown, very faintly purplish: first run only of 4073.

Variations in brown paint, one of the colors most frequently used by Lehmann, have been very subtle and are hard to describe.   The browns most commonly used in major body components have a bright, decidedly orange hue.
1. Tan: 4047 cask, circa 1981.
2. Orange-brown: latest version of 2040 crocodile and 2045.
3. Brown: 4067 (first D.&R.G. version), 2040 crocodile, 3007 (circa 1979) and perhaps some of the early 2010 and 2020 locomotives.
4. Chocolate brown: 20526 Schmidt Bakery set.
5. Red-brown: latest 4061.
6. Very dark brown: 2010 (circa 1980).

WHITES AND CREAMS

White plastic has almost the identical tonality as white paint, but its finish is duller.

Whites and beiges have been used on two-tone paint schemes on both locomotives and coaches and several freight cars.

White paint usually has a glossy finish, such as on the last version of the 4032L.

Light cream plastic: creamy off-white, clearly more colorful than the whites above: long used on two-tone cars 3011, 3012 and 3064.

Dark cream paint, less white, darker and much yellower than #1, over which it is sprayed: latest 3011, 3012 and 3064.

GRAYS

Gray plastic appears in two shades.
1. Dull light gray: early 4045, 4001 and most early roofs.
2. Dull medium gray: used on some roofs and the 2060 series chassis.

Gray paint to-date has only been used as a secondary color, as for roofs.
1. Glossy light gray: used on some early locomotives roofs, 2050.
2. Glossy medium gray: used briefly in the mid-1970s.
3. Glossy greenish-gray: currently used on most roofs.

BLACK

Black plastic has a glossy finish: it was used on many early 0-4-0 locomotive cabs; and currently is used on most 0-4-0 locomotive boilers. It also is seen on early rolling stock chassis and the 4000 flatcar.

Only one flat black paint has been used on most rolling stock chassis, such as the latest 4040B.

Chapter VI
Passenger Coaches and Baggage Cars

Although the larger cars are impressive, the small 300 mm passenger cars, representing prototypes approximately 22 feet long, have a powerful diminutive appeal. A single man may switch such a car without an engine, simply putting his weight against a handrail and leaning on it until it begins to roll slowly.

NOTE: For a more detailed description of body and roof types please refer to Chapter V — Rolling Stock Descriptions.

Passenger coach designations are as follows:

A, B, C — first, second, third class

D, Pw — Luggage van

K — Narrow gauge vehicle (DB)

Post — Post (Mail) van

i — with open gangway between coaches

0 — with covered gangway between coaches

p — Express coach with central gangway

/s — Narrow gauge of the OBB (Austrian railway)

4 — Bogie wagon with four axles (of the OBB)

Designating and additional letters denote the type of passenger wagon, e.g. Ci/s is a third class, narrow gauge passenger coach with open gangway, of the OBB.

All 300 mm passenger cars with platforms have SW2 railings (Solid Wall with square side gates) if produced through 1978, and SA2 railings (Solid wall with Accordion-gated aisleway and square side gates) if produced from 1979 to 1986.

Window frames have been produced in yellow, brown and red. The earliest produced yellow frames are a light lemon-yellow (1969-1970) but later changed (around 1971) to a deeper orange-yellow color which is still currently used.

Anniversary cars commemorate the four years subsequent to the 100 year anniversary of the Lehmann Company. All have an embossed 3007 as identification. The cars were sold for use with the 1981 Red Jubilee Train Set 20801 (or the Blue Train 20301BZ). All are 300 mm long.

1982: 1982, 101st anniversary four-wheel coach, with unpainted light cream Simulated Metal SM2(B) body (four windows on each side, raised corner seams and window sill seam); red silk-screened details and lettering; red window frames; Medium-Arched MA3 roof (six seams, three vents); filigree roof supports; Type 2 frame markings. **65**

1983: 1983, 102nd anniversary four-wheel coach, with two-tone light cream and dark blue Simulated Metal SM2(B) body, same as 1982 (four windows on each side, vertical corner seams and one horizontal seam level with window bases); gold silk-screened details and lettering on the blue lower portion and blue lettering on the cream upper portion; Medium-Arched MA3 roof, same as 1982 (six seams, three vents); filigree roof supports; orange-yellow window frames; Type 2 frame markings. More scarce than 1982 car. **100**

1984: 1984, 103rd anniversary four-wheel coach, with a completely dark blue Simulated Metal SM2(B) body, same type as 1981 and 1982; orange-yellow window frames; Medium-Arched MA3 roof, same as 1981 and 1982 (six seams, three vents); filigree roof supports; body markings and lettering silk-screened in gold; Type 3 frame markings. **100**

1985: 1985, 104th anniversary four-wheel car, a painted dark blue 3019 postal wagon with markings which most closely match 3019(E), but markings and window grill edges have gold finish. On the false doors toward end of car opposite brakeman's platform is an "1881-1985" filigree

logo. The car has 3019/1 metal wheels; 3031 tail lamps; wiring outlets at each end; same Medium-Arched MA3 roof as the preceding cars in this series (six seams, three vents); filigree roof supports; Type 3 frame markings. Came with extra coupler, 2040/2, in 1985. **100**

3000: 1969-81, Bi/s four-wheel second or third class coach of the Lower Austrian Railway (Niederosterreichischen Landesbahn). Painted or unpainted, Simulated Wood-paneled SW1 body (four windows on each side); most came with a Low-Arched roof (six seams, two vents); but some may have been sold with a Clerestory roof which has six small windows and five covered vents on each side, B. Cage comment; glued on metal "LGB" plaque on each side; listed in catalogue from 1968 to 1982; length 300 mm. A closed platform prototype was also proposed but never produced; R. Enners comment. Also see 3006.

This 3000 coach has early style roof vents. A. Rudman Collection.

(A) 1968-70, dark brown unpainted body with light lemon-yellow window frames; second class; no markings on chassis frames; Low-Arched LA1 roof (light gray without shading; two small vents); second class (2 and 2); Solid Wall SW2 railing. **150**

(B) 1969-70, same as (A), but third class; light yellow window frames. **150**

(C) 1971-77, same as (A), but third class; orange-yellow window frames. **120**

(D) 1976, body unpainted pinkish-red, 3000 ID number, no LGB plaque on raised area of body; orange-yellow window frames. Made for Metro Co. of W. Germany; W. Richter comment. **NRS**

(E) 1978-79, body painted red-brown over brown plastic; SA2 railing (Solid wall with Accordion-gated aisleway); second class; no markings on chassis frames; Low-Arched LA1 roof (light gray roof with shading; two black vents). **90**

(F) 1978-79, same as (E), but third class. **90**

(G) 1980-81, same as (E), but with improved paint job; Type 1 frame markings; known only in second class. **75**

NOTE: Four versions produced for Primus painted bright red or green; B. Cage comment.

(H) 1979-80, same as (E), but body painted red, second class in Arabic numbers, made for LGB or Primus. **90**

(I) 1979-80, same as (E), but body painted red, third class in Arabic numbers, made for LGB or Primus. **90**

(J) 1979-80, same as (E), but body painted green, second class in Arabic numbers, made for Primus only. **120**

(K) 1979-80, same as (E), but body painted green, third class in Arabic numbers, made for Primus only. **120**

3006: 1982-86, four-wheel passenger coach of the "Dodge City & Great Western Railroad". Similar to 3000, yellow Simulated Wood-paneled SW1

Often misidentified as the 3000 from which it is derived, 3006 retains its European air in spite of its American label, "Dodge City and Great Western Railroad".

body (four windows) with 3000 or 3006 ID number; green and red trim; brown window frames; painted and shaded Low-Arched LA1 roof (six seams, two vents); no markings on chassis frames; length 300 mm; introduced in 1982 as part of set 20701DC, but first pictured in 1983-84 catalogue; version (C) is the only one sold separately. Also see 3006BP.

(A) 1982, first class; 3000 ID number; smooth, untextured roof; sold with 20701DC.   **NSS**
(B) 1982, same as (A), but with 3006 ID number; sold with 20701DC.   **NSS**
(C) 1982-86, similar to (B), but has textured roof.   **CP**
(D) 1982, similar to (A), but second class, sold with 20701DC.   **NSS**

These three 3007s vary in color. The oldest of this group, with its pre-1979 coupler and Solid Wall railing, is at the top; the newest and current issue is at bottom right. Note that the classes are different on all three. For the very earliest version of this car, compare these wide-windowed versions, the only issue since 1975 and the basis of most passenger cars in limited edition sets, to the narrow-windowed version in the photo found on page 49. C. Colwell Collection.

A group of Lehmann passenger classics: at top, 3007(B), still with the tall narrow windows of the first version, in contrast to the squarish windows that typify the car in its many liveries over the last dozen years; middle left, the original dark brown livery of the vertically paneled 3000; lower left, a 3040 whose seamless roof and yellow upper window shade/vents were superceded in 1979. Middle right and lower right, two restfully unlettered baggage wagons, 3020 and 3019, distinguished by their respectively Low-Arched and Medium-Arched roofs. Notice the absence of roof-edge shading from the two gray roofs, suggesting a date before 1976. C. Colwell Collection.

(E) 1982, similar to (B), but second class, sold with 20701DC.   **NSS**

3006BP: 1984, four-wheel second class passenger coach of the "Buffalo Pass Scalplock & Denver Railroad" train set 20301BP. Same style coach as 3000, Simulated Wood-paneled SW1 body (four windows); orange-yellow frames; yellow "2" on sides of body; yellow horizontal stripe along body just beneath window sills; yellow road name along body above windows; slightly-raised brass-colored "LGB" logo plaque on each side; Low-Arched LA1 roof (six seams, two vents); Type 3 frame markings.   **NSS**

3007: 1971-86, Bci/s four-wheel coach issued in first, first/second, second or second/third class versions of the Zillertal Railway. Body various shades of brown with light lemon-yellow or orange-yellow window frames (all versions have 3007 ID number); hand-painted Simulated Metal SM1 and SM2(A) or (B) bodies (four windows each side) with deep yellow window panels, three horizontal bars over lower glass of door windows; Medium-Arched roofs. Most pieces lack filigree roof supports which are generally

turned towards inside of coach, often turned around later by store or purchaser; but the original had no filigree, and Eberhard Richter didn't like shipping the standard mold end with empty slots, and so filled them with the reversed filigree. Sometimes defective filigree pieces were used for this purpose; J. Barton comment. Also see 1982, 1983, 1984, 3007BE, 3007BZ, 3007HS, 3007L, 3007LJ, 3007MF, 3007MS, 3007PB, 3011D, 3013PB and 3150.

(A) 1971-72, third class with Roman numerals on raised number-boards; unpainted straw-colored SM1 body (five vertical and three horizontal seams, tall narrow windows); no frame markings; white "Zillertalbahn" logo on black plaque nearly the length of two windows; MA1 roof (smooth).   **135**

(B) 1972-73, same as (A), but with Arabic numbers; either first, second or third class.   **135**

(C) 1974-76, second/third class with Arabic numbers on raised number-boards; straw-colored SM2(A) body (vertical corner seams and one horizontal seam; squarish windows); smaller white "Zillertalbahn" logo on raised black plaque; "ABi/S 1" in right side corners of body; no frame markings; Medium-Arched MA1 roof (no seams) or MA2 (six seams). **80**

(D) 1977-78, same as (C), but painted a deep caramel color; no white detail markings in right side corners of body; no frame markings. **75**

(E) 1979-83, second class with Arabic numbers reduced in size; painted-on, black "Zillertalbahn" on raised plaque with white border, "Bi 1/S" replaces earlier markings in right side corners of SM2(A) body (raised boards or plaques; vertical corner seams, one horizontal seam); Type 1 frame markings. **50**

(F) 1983-85, same as (E), but SM2(B) body (unraised number-boards/logo plaques; vertical corner seams and one horizontal seam). **CP**

(G) 1986, first and second class; decidedly reddish brown; smaller unraised "Zillertalbahn" plaque with no white outline, tiny no smoking emblems (red X over cigarette) at side corners. MA3 roof (six seams, three vents). **CP**

3007BE: 1985. A four-wheel coach for the "Bundesgartenschau Express" train set made for the landscaping company from West Berlin bearing the same name. This car has a Simulated Metal SM2(B) body (unraised boards or plaques; vertical corner seams and one horizontal seam; also has a 3007 identification number), painted navy blue with orange-yellow window frames and late frame markings. The body markings are all in gold paint (gold filigree markings are the same as on the 1984 anniversary car) and include "Bundesgartenschau Express" just below roof line. The company's logo, a child-like flower, is in the center of each side of the body below the windows with the markings "Berlin" and "1985" to its left and right respectively. Medium-Arched MA3 roof (six seams, three vents); interior has five sets of medium brown bench seats on a blue floor. **NSS**

3007BZ: 1982-83, similar to the 3007 (has 3007 ID number), but with painted dark blue Simulated Metal SM2(B) body (unraised boards or plaques; vertical corner seams and one horizontal seam); red trim and lettering; red window frames; sold with the Blue Train set 20301BZ; Medium-Arched MA3 roof (six seams, three vents); gold "DER BLAUE ZUG . THE BLUE TRAIN . LE TRAIN BLEU" over windows, blue "LGB" with gold-painted logo shape centered under windows. May also have come with silver trim and lettering; M. Richter comment. **55**

3007HS: 1984, similar to the 3007 (has 3007 ID number), but with painted red smooth-sided Simulated Metal SM2(B) body (unraised boards or plaques; vertical corner seams and one horizontal seam); orange-yellow window frames; an orange, red and white horizontal stripe along side about 38 mm below window; no other markings on body; Medium-Arched MA3 roof (six seams, three vents); and the usual SA2 railing (Solid wall with Accordion-gated aisleway; operating square side gates; sold with "Freizeit Hobby Spiel" train set 20513. **NSS**

3007L: 1983, anniversary car for the 100th year jubilee of Lutgenau Hobby and Train company of West Germany. Simulated Metal SM2(B) body (unraised boards or plaques; corner seams and one horizontal seam), with 3007 ID number, red window frames; Type 2 frame markings; Medium-Arched charcoal gray MA2 roof (six seams) or MA3 roof (six seams, three vents) with darker shading; very similar to the 1982 101st anniversary LGB car, but blue striping and graphics with "100 Jahre" and "Lutgenau" rather than Lehmann inside wreath; date at left of wreath is "1876" with "1986" to the right. **450**

3007LJ: 1981, similar to the 3007(F) (has 3007 ID number), but with painted cranberry body with gold trim and jubilee lettering; sold with the 100 Anniversary Jubilee Red Train set 20801; Medium-Arched MA3 roof (six seams, three vents). **NRS**

3007MF: 1984, uncatalogued; Marshall Field & Company four-wheel coach. Similar to 3007(F) (has 3007 ID number), but with body painted dark green with gold pin stripes and graphics; "Marshall Field & Company" above orange-yellow window frames; "1852", "1984" at center side of body below windows with company herald in between; Medium-Arched MA3 roof (six seams, three vents); filigree roof supports; Type 3 frame markings; sold with set 20301MF but boxed separately in a 3007MF window box as well; less than 1200 made. **100**

3007MS: 1985-86, four-wheel coach of the limited production commemorative set for Modelleisenbahn Schweiger of West Germany.

(A) 1985, yellow-painted Simulated Metal SM2(B) body (unraised boards or plaques; corner seams and one horizontal seam), with 3007 identification number, red window frames; Medium-Arched gray MA3 roof (six seams,

three vents), with black shading; filigree roof supports; SA2 railing (accordion-gates); black "Stadteexpress Nurnberg-Furth, Jubilaumsausgabe (Eisenbahnjahr 1985)" along roof line on both sides of body with an olive-green horizontal stripe just below it (stripe has heralds at each end); body panel below windows is decorated with horizontal olive-green stripes along with "Schweiger" (in red and black) and "LGB" (in black) logos. "1835", "1985" and a figure of the Adler locomotive are lithographed at the lower center of each side. "(150 Jahre Deutsche Eisenbahnen)" and heralds are on an olive-green stripe at lower edge of each body side; Type 3 frame markings. **NSS**

(B)1986, olive-green SM2(B) body. Further details pending release of car. Sold with set 20529. **NSS**

3007PB: 1984, uncatalogued; a four-wheel 3007 series coach (has 3007ID number) with SM2(B) body (unraised boards or plaques; corner seams and one horizontal seam), painted in dark green (same color as 3007MF or 3070, etc.); orange-yellow window frames; body markings include: a white-painted-on plaque with "MC Modellbahn-Center Sonderzug" above "Zell a. See-Krimml" all in black lettering; two small, square-shaped no smoking signs in white, red and black on each side next to boarding gates; left lower corner markings are "(—8,10m—)", above "6,4t 28Pl Av-P5t", above "Bi/S 3850"; right lower corner markings are

2M	1	2	3	4	5	6	7	8	9	10	11	12		REV	Z	22	8	82
					:									NR			8	84

MA3 roof (six seams, three vents); Type 3 frame markings. **NSS**

This early 3008 is based on an Austrian prototype. Discontinued about 1978, the latest models were issued with accordion end gates (SA2 railing) and late (L1) wheels. A. Rudman Collection.

3008: 1971-78, second or third class BCSi Austrian railway coach (Landesbahnen). Hand-painted green lower body with white upper body; orange-yellow window frames.

(A) 1971-74, Simulated Metal SM1 body (five vertical and three horizontal seams); LGB logo on raised brass plaque on each side; no detail lettering on frames; usually second class with Roman numerals; Medium-Arched roof. **65**

(B) 1975-76, third class with Arabic numerals on raised number-boards; Simulated Metal SM2(A) body (raised plaques; corner seams and one horizontal seam); plaques have no lettering; no detail lettering on frames; Medium-Arched MA2 roof (six seams, no vents). **120**

(C) 1976-78, same as(A), but second class with Arabic numbers; early style wheels; the usual Solid Wall SW2 railings (square side gates). V. Winn Collection. **100**

(D) 1976-78, same as (A), but Medium-Arched MA1 roof (no seams). **100**

(E) 1978, Simulated Metal SM3 body (five vertical, four horizontal seams; raised plaques); Medium-Arched MA2 roof (six seams, no vents); V. Winn collection.

3009: 1971-73, four-wheel second or third class "BCi/S" passenger coach of the Murtalbahn Railway. Medium-Arched charcoal gray-painted (slightly shaded) MA1 roof (no seams); same basic coach as 3008(A), except in solid unpainted dark or medium green; orange-yellow framed windows in SM1 body (five vertical, three horizontal seams); metal axles; the usual black filigree roof supports; length 300 mm.

3009 was only produced for three years, 1971-1973. It has a seamless, Medium-Arched MA1 roof. A. Rudman Collection.

(A) Roman numerals.   350
(B) Arabic numbers.   350

3010: 1969-86, second class or third class Ci/S Salzkammergut Local Railway coach. Hand-painted green; light lemon-yellow or orange-yellow window frames; Clerestory CL1 roof (six windows, five vents on each side); filigree supports; length 300 mm.

(A) 1969-70, second class with Roman numerals on raised number-boards painted light green or unpainted dark green; light lemon-yellow window frames in Simulated Metal SM1 body (five vertical, three horizontal seams); no detail lettering on frames; raised brass "LGB" plaque on each side.   85

(B) 1970-73, same as (A), but in third class. This and subsequent versions have not light lemon-yellow, but orange-yellow ("orange"; B. Roth comment) window frames.   85

(C) 1974-77, same as (A), but in second or third class with Arabic numbers.   75

(D) 1978-80, same as (A), but in third class with Arabic numbers; Type 1 frame markings; shiny finished medium green-painted body.   65

(E) 1978-80, same as (A), but with Type 1 frame markings; third class in Arabic numbers.   55

(F) 1981-82, second class in Arabic numbers on raised number-boards; Simulated Metal SM3 body (five vertical, four horizontal seams); Type 1 frame markings; "Nichtraucher" signs next to class numbers; detail marking in upper and lower left-hand corner of sides.   50

(G) 1983-84, same as (F), but first class, Type 2 frame markings.   45

(H) 1983-86, same as (G), in third class.   CP

3011: 1969-86, second or third class four-wheel coach of the North German Island Railway; two-tone red or cranberry and light cream or dark cream body; Clerestory roof (six windows, five vents); filigree supports; raised metal "LGB" logo glued to each side; length 300 mm.

(A) 1969-70, second class with Roman numerals on raised number-boards; cranberry and light cream Simulated Metal SM1 body (five vertical, three horizontal seams); light lemon-yellow window frames; no frame markings; no extra marking detail on body other than class designation and raised "LGB" logo. Some came with beveled glass windows; B. Roth comment. Confirmation requested.   100

(B) 1971-74, same as (A), but third class; body painted red and white; orange-yellow window frames.   85

(C) 1974-75, same as (A), but in red and white.   75

(D) 1976-78, same as (B), but second class with Arabic numbers. 65

(E) 1976-78, same as (C), but third class in Arabic numbers.   65

(F) 1979-80, same as (C), but third class Arabic numbers; SM3 body (four horizontal seams), painted red and white; Type 1 frame markings.   50

(G) 1981-86, second class with Arabic numbers; SM3 body (four horizontal seams) painted red and white (1985-86, dark cream); Type 1 or 2 frame markings; body has "Nichtraucher" signs near class numbers, black spec markings in upper left-hand side corner; white spec markings in lower left-hand side corner.   CP

3011D: 1985. Four-wheel coach built to commemorate the 1100 year history of Duisburg, West Germany. This coach has a red-painted Simulated Metal body and probably has 3007 identification number, orange-yellow window frames, Medium-Arched roof and Type 2 frame markings (at least on the prototype). Markings on the body are all in gold paint and include: "Jubilaums-Express" above windows; an eagle and castle herald at center of panel below windows; "1100 Jahre Duisburg 833-1983" to the right of herald and the signatures "Josef Krings" and "Herbert Kramer" above their printed names and titles ("Oberbergermeister" and "Oberstadtdirecktur" respectively) to the left. Only 500 of these coaches were made as commissioned by the Lutgenau Company of West Germany; Mr. Zeck provided a photograph of this car.   165

3012: 1969-86, same basic four-wheel coach as the 3011, but with blue rather than red paint on lower portion of body; Clerestory CL1 roof (six windows, five vents); filigree roof supports; since 1979, only available with set 20301; length 300 mm.

(A) 1969-70, second class with Roman numerals; SM1 body (five vertical, three horizontal seams), with light lemon-yellow window frames; painted blue and light cream; no frame markings. A few came with beveled glass windows; B. Roth comment. Confirmation requsted.   100

(B) 1971-74, similar to (A), but in third class.   80

(C) 1975-79, second class with Arabic numbers.   75

(D) 1979-80, third class with Arabic numbers; blue and white.   60

A descendant of the earliest passenger car in the Lehmann line, 3010 has gone through several color and class variations. Since 1981, it has had four (SM3 body) rather than three (SM1) horizontal seams, but always five vertical seams.

At the top of this group with Clerestory or "Clearstory" roofs, named for the windows in a story (level) that clears the lower portion of the roof, the red-bottomed 3011 and the blue-bottomed 3012; they have been in set 20301, with a recent slight color variation, since 1968, although 3012 is no longer issued separately. Bottom left, a dark green 3010 (the lighter green of the photo found on page 51); a darker, cranberry red 3011 at right. Light yellow frames identify the bottom two as quite old, in contrast to the duller and more orange-yellow frames above. C. Colwell Collection.

(E) 1978-80, same as (D), but in second class with Arabic numbers. **60**

(F) 1981-86, second class with Arabic numbers; body like (A), but type SM3 (four horizontal seams); black spec markings in upper left-hand side corner; white dimension markings in lower left-hand side corner; "Nichtraucher" near class numbers; Type 1 or 2 frame markings. **NSS**

3013: 1973-86, four-wheel Bi/s dining car of the Steyrtal Railway. blue-painted Simulated Metal SM2(A) or (B) body; with 3013 ID number; orange-yellow window frames; interior furnishings for restaurant facilities; Low-Arched LA3 roof (six seams, two vents); filigree supports; length 300 mm.

(A) 1973-76, Simulated Metal SM2(A) body (vertical corner seams, one horizontal seam; raised boards/plaques); painted medium blue with yellow-gold markings. Raised "Brau Ag" plaque with standing lions on black background is glued into depression on each side of body; no frame markings. **115**

(B) 1976-78, same as (A), but with larger raised "Brau Ag" plaque with painted, not raised, lettering; plaque lacks black background; Type 1 frame markings. **75**

(C) 1978-80, body painted darker blue; same body type, color and graphics as (B), but "Brau Ag" plaque is larger. **70**

(D) 1981-85, like C, but yellow-gold markings; SM2(B) body (non-raised, plaque painted on); no frame markings. **CP**

3013LJ: 1981, similar to 3013, but has 3007 ID number on card end; upper half painted white or cream, lower half red (cranberry) with gold trim and jubilee markings; "SPEISEWAGEN" over windows; orange-yellow window and end door panel frames; "1881" and "1981" with gold oval chain with "100 JAHRE/LEHMANN" on side; SM2(B) body (corner seams, one horizontal seam; plaques, if present, not raised); MA3 roof (six seams, three vents); sold only with set 20801. **NSS**

3013PB: 1984, uncatalogued; Pinzgauer Bahn Austrian diner. Orange-yellow window frames; 3007 ID number on SM2(B) body (unraised boards or plaques, with corner seams and one horizontal seam), which is painted

medium blue (about the same as 3007BZ or 3013(D)); the words "PINZGA SCHENKE" in one-half inch tall yellow letters across each side below windows; left lower corner markings are "Barwagen" above "5902" above "Av5t :5,6t:" above

2M	1	2	3	4	5	6	7	8	9	10	11	12
					:							

right lower corner markings are

	REV	Z	22	7	82
	NR			7	84

LA1 roof ; Type 3 frame markings. **NSS**

3014: 1979-82, Type C four-wheel coach of the Suddeutschen Eisenbahngesellschaft, which also runs several lines into North East Germany. Light green Simulated Metal SM3 body (five vertical, four horizontal seams); orange-yellow window frames; raised white flying wheel logo on each side; white dimension markings in upper left-hand side corner; LA3 roof (six seams, two vents); corner posts from roof to platforms; Type 1 frame markings; length 300 mm.

(A) 1979-80, second class with Arabic numbers on raised number-boards; white "nichtraucher" signs. Also with double-stacked vents and "32 platze" in lower left corner; C. Colwell comment. **80**

(B) 1980-82, third class with Arabic numbers on raised number-boards, with red "raucher" signs; double-stacked vents; "32 platze" in lower left corner. **70**

3015: 1979-86, second class Bavarian four-wheel coach of a south German local railway (has 3015 ID number). LA3 roof (six seams, two vents); filigree supports; metal grab-handle supports from roof to platforms; blue and white Simulated Metal SM3 body (five vertical, four horizontal seams); raised number-boards and logo plaques; orange-yellow window frames; length 300 mm.

(A) 1979-81, metal "LGB" plaque on each side and class numbers are the only body markings; Type 1 frame markings. **70**

(B) 1982-83, similar to (A), but with the addition of left-end side detail markings and "Nichtraucher" signs; Type 1 or 2 frame markings. **CP**

Because of its inclusion, with 3012, in the basic passenger set, 3011 is one of the most common coaches. For a very small fee, visitors to the Austrian Zillertal Railway can be the engineer on a fare-hauling 0-4-0T pulling this coach and its blue-bottomed mate. The model's striking Clerestory CL1 roof is unpopular at the factory because it is awkward to assemble.

(C) 1983-86, similar to (B), but with winged wheel logo and "LGB 3015" replacing metal side plaque. **CP**

NOTE: 3019. Cars built circa 1973 and perhaps earlier had a divider plate on the inside floor of the car just out of the doorway on the blind end, used to keep in place batteries installed in the last versions of the 3019 and perhaps 3020 lacking metal wheels for power for the three-volt car lighting system used until the introduction of 3019(E) with metal wheel pickup system. These cars also have receptacles for 3030 wires though they lack metal wheels. The supports for the vertical divider plates were also molded into the floors of all the later 300 mm boxcars, i.e. 4030, etc. V. Winn comment.

3019(3019N): 1971-86, four-wheel parcels/mail van PW Post of the former KPEV with luggage space and special compartment for mail (all have 3019 ID number). Opening sliding doors; Medium-Arched MA1 or MA2 roofs; typical freight, not passenger, railings — first, type SW1 (Solid Wall, triangular side gates), then FA4 (Frame of Angle iron, no side gates); as brake van for passenger or goods trains, later models are fitted with 3019/1 metal wheel sets and current 3019/3 brushes and pickup for tail and internal lighting; earliest edition completely lacked painted detail, markings or lettering and was not lighted; length 300 mm.
(A) 1971-74, 3019; plain very dark unpainted green body; brakeman's platform with SW1 railings (Solid Wall, triangular side gates); no painted numbers, lettering, or decals on body or frame; no lights; Medium-Arched MA1 roof (no seams or vents); Type E1 plastic wheels; small embossed "LGB" logo (on upper right corner of front end and on upper forward window); letter drop slot, envelope plaque and curled bugle are all embossed on lower portion of last panel at end of brakeman's platform. **250**
(B) 1972, 3019; same as (A), in slightly lighter unpainted green. **NRS**
(C) 1972-73, 3019; medium brown unpainted body with exactly the same detail markings as in (A); this piece was made for Primus Company by Lehmann. **200**
(D) 1975-76, 3019N; same body color as (A), but differs with changes including the addition of a simulated, hinged, non-opening door between the sliding side door and the end opposite the brakeman's platform; MA2 roof (six seams, no vents); addition of filigree roof supports; 3031 taillights; 4000/1 plastic Type 2 wheels; lighting outlet over forward door; lighting current picked up via kits 3030, rather than wheels; details on sides include painted orange-yellow window frames; white-lettered "LGB" and "3019N" on sliding doors, covering the height of one slat, KPEV eagle emblem in upper rear corner; printed letter slot reads "Post Nach" and "Briefkasten"; "Post" in white letters on black plaque above non-opening side door, door composed of wood-grain identical to body; "Pw-Posti" above embossed "LGB" logo in upper forward corner, "Av-P 5.ot", "Lastgr. 3,1t", "5,ot" and "11,2m2" in lower forward corner on fifth through third slots from bottom. **100**

Originally issued with raised plaques, the 3013 authentically diminutive diner has the rather square windows of 3007, unlike the narrower windows of most other 300 mm long passenger cars.

Although it is unlikely that a prototype would have both corner posts and filigree brackets to support its roof, Lehmann disovered from their experience with 3007 how popular the brackets are: People who received cars with filigree turned inward, used simply to fill the slots (the prototype had no such supports), promptly turned them around. 3015 displays its unnecessary brackets.

(E) 1977, 3019N; same as (D), but with 3019/1 metal wheels; 3019/3 current brushes for lighting.　　　　　　　　　　　　　　　**100**

(F) 1978, 3019; slightly lighter green body than (E); "LGB" and "3019N" markings on sliding doors smaller than (D) or (E), covering less than height of one slat; otherwise very similar to (E).　　　　　　　　**85**

(G) 1979-80, 3019; same as (D), but with separate mail section with interior lighting; 3019/1 metal wheels with 3019/3 current pickups; simulated hinged, non-opening side door smooth, like door to brakeman's platform; SA1 railing to brakeman's platform (Solid wall with Accordion-gated aisleway, triangular gates).　　　　　　　　　　　**100**

(H) 1980-81, same as (G), but with Type 1 frame markings.　　**68**

(I) 1982-83, 3019; same as (C), but with painted dark green body; FA4 railings (open Frame of Angle iron; no side gates to platform); changes in painted detail include square white computer markings on each corner, level with the fourth slot from bottom, no "N" with "3019" on sliding door, "5,ot" and "11,2m2" reduced in size and moved up to the seventh and eighth slots from bottom; additional detail includes "3019" in upper forward corner beneath embossed "LGB" logo, "Hz1." in lower forward corner, white detail markings in the lower rear corner and a yellow curled trumpet on hinged, smooth side door.　　　　　　　　　　　　**75**

(J) 1983-86, 3019; same as (E), but with changes in detail on sliding door including two-tone yellow and black "LGB" logo, "Pwgh" added on slot below "3019" and a black "chalkboard" with "von" and "nach" on lower part of door; curled bugle reversed on both sides.　　　　　**CP**

3020: 1969-74, four-wheel baggage car of the Pinzgau Local Railway. Virtually identical in color and form to the earliest 3019 (see 3019(A) and (B)) but has 3020 ID number and some came with a light gray roof (six seams, two vents) and black filigree roof supports.

(A) 1969-70, unpainted dark green Simulated Wood body; black frame.　**280**

(B) 1971-74, unpainted slightly lighter green body.　　　　　　**400**

3040: 1971-86, four-wheel Ci/S second or third class passenger coach of the Mixnitz-St. Erhard Railway. Metal corner grab-handles/roof supports from platform steps to roof; off-center aisle separating single seats from double; green hand-painted Simulated Wood-paneled SW2 body (six windows each side, one window and off-set door on ends—the only instance of this asymmetrical arrangement); orange-yellow window frames; clear tieback curtains incised in windows; length 300 mm.

(A) 1971-73, class numbers in Roman numerals; the usual early passenger SW2 railing (Solid Wall, with square side gates); early wheels; SW2(A) body (tall windows split at top by yellow horizontal dividers with yellow louvered shade vents); no frame markings; a flattened seamless type TA1 roof which is tapered toward edges and ends.　　　　　　　　**120**

(B) 1974-77, same as (A), but with second class in Arabic numbers; and later wheels.　　　　　　　　　　　　　　　　　**100**

(C) 1974-78, same as (A), but unpainted green body; later wheels; second class in Arabic numbers; gold "LGB" on black.　　　　　**100**

(D) 1979-86, same as (A), but SW2(B) body (shorter windows; panes divided at top, orange-yellow window frames separated from louver-type shade vents which are green and molded with the body); white pin stripes around sides below windows; TA2 roof (tapered like TA1, but seven seams); later wheels; "LBM-St.E." in left lower corner, "C 1" in right lower corner; Type 1 or 2 frame markings; may have had second or third class in Arabic numbers.　　　　　　　　　　　　　　　**CP**

3050: 1971-86, third class compartment coach of North German Island Railway (ex-Prussian). Dark green body with both smoking and non-smoking compartments; all compartment doors open; no end platforms or doors; windows in orange-yellow inset frames; compartment walls with

The first 3019 baggage wagon was unpainted plastic, unlettered but for the number stamped into the end. 3019 was produced from 1971 to 1974. Occasionally, as with the 3006, 3007, 3013PB, 3150, 4031, 4032 and 4034, Lehmann has marketed and catalogued a car under a different number from the one stamped on it. A. Rudman Collection.

Closely resembling the early 3019, 3020 differed primarily in its Low-Arched LA3 roof, rather than the Medium-Arched MA1 roof of 3019. A. Rudman Collection.

one-piece bench sets; Clerestory gray CL2 roof (eight windows, four vents); length 300 mm. Note the foot plates along the complete length of the body which enable the conductor to enter individual compartments even during the journey.

(A) 1971-73, unpainted dark green grab-irons same color as body; no brake pipes; E1 early wheels; step with six supports; white Roman numerals on doors without black background; forward compartment second or third class; cone-shaped roof vents; embossed round plastic green-colored door handles. **165**

(B) 1974-78, third class only; white Roman numerals on black background; red smoking and white non-smoking signs; embossed round plastic green door handles; grab-irons painted black; cone-shaped roof vents; only five step supports; brake pipe present on end with steps; E2 wheels. About 1975 some of these cars were built with the round silver rivet door handles; no frame markings; painted grab-rails but no brake pipe; D. Weiler comment: confirmed C. Colwell. The silver rivets are the same as used on smoke box doors. **130**

(C) 1979-80, same as (B), but painted dark green with round brass or silver-colored rivet-head door handles and detail lettering on frames. **85**

(D) 1981-86, same as (B), but with elongated, gold-colored door handles; lettering details on each side include "3050", "KC2", "5,64t", "40 P1", "6,75m" and "Hbr" in upper left corners and "Nhz" in lower left corner; frame lettering slightly different. **CP**

3060: 1971-80, 1986, Barmer second and third class eight-wheel mountain railway coach. Gray Clerestory CL3 roof (eight windows, no vents, stove stacks), with shading; filigree roof supports; SW3 railings (Solid Wall, solid operating side gates); four pairs of windows on each side and opening centered end doors, either solid 3000/1 or spoked 4000/1 wheels; Length 420 mm.

(A) 1971-3, medium green with yellow-gold pin stripes on sides; embossed "3060" in upper left-hand corner of body end at platform; no lettering on frames; no steam regulator on exterior ends; may not have been produced.

NRS

(B) 1971-80, same as (A), but with embossed steam regulators; etched curtains on windows; gold "II" in panel under first two windows, "III" in panel under last two. **150**

(C) 1971-72, same as (B), but in dark brown. **185**

(D) 1985-86, medium green body; same body and frame markings as 3061(C), except that "3060" replaces "3061" in upper left-hand corner. **CP**

3061: 1981-84, same basic coach as 3060.

(A) 1973-80, same as 3060(C), but with dark olive-brown body; "3060" identification on end of body. **165**

(B) 1981, similar to (A), but with "3061" identification marking on end of body, embossed steam regulators; shiny, light gray roof with shading. **80**

(C) 1982, same as (B), but with dark gray roof with shading. **85**

(D) 1983-84, same as (C), but with white "3061", "BCiP", "14t", "32P1", "9,5m" and "Hbr" in upper left-hand corner of sides; "Abst d Drehz 5.0m", "Achs Unt Bww Mst 7.3.86", "Nhhz", "Einh Dyn Bel" and "N Unt 1.12.88" on frames. **70**

3062: 1974-86, eight-wheel B4iP/s through-train coach of the Austrian Federal Railways in service on the Pinzgauer Local Railway; similar to the type used on the Maria-Zeller railway, the Murtal railway, the Zillertal railway and the Steyrtal railway. Simulated Metal SM4(A) or (B) body (six non-sliding windows, two recessed doors open); rigid folding gates across vestibule end doors at both ends; three compartments with interior furnishings. Medium-Arched MA4 roof (seven seams); restroom has wash basin and hinged toilet seat; length 460 mm.

(A) 1974-75, unpainted all-gray roof; painted dark green SM4(A) body (door hinge pinions and pinion holes are small, 1-1/2 mm in diameter); narrow folding gate and step at ends; window frames same color as body; doors without working handles; limited body markings; "15,ot", "50P1", "Av-Pi3t", "B4iSp" and "3062" on plaque in a relatively deep depression at lower left-hand side corner of body; frame markings at four intervals along frame directly beneath windows two, three, four and five. **120**

(B) 1976, same as (A), but with orange-yellow window frames. **120**

(C) 1976-77, same as (B), but frame markings placed only beneath windows two and five. **100**

(D) 1977-78, same as (C), but with medium green body. . **100**

In 1979 the orange-yellow window frames of 3040 were separated from the vents above them, to which they had always been joined in one casting. Its unique off-center end door and aisle, dividing a row of single seats from a row of double, and its rare Tapered-Arch roof give this car its distinctive old-fashioned flavor.

A full-length step provides conductor and intrepid passengers access from compartment to compartment while the aisle-less 3050 is in motion. Earlier versions had smaller roof vents and several variations of door handles.

(E) 1979-80, similar to (B), but doors with working brass-colored handles; second and third class markings added. **CP**

(F) 1980, custom painted orange body with black pin stripes; flat black-painted roof; made for LGB Big Train Operator's club raffle; gangways added; only two made. Not Lehmann production. **NSS**

(G) 1981-86, SM4(B) body (door hinge pinions and holes same as (A), but plaque markings in lower left-hand side corner only slightly depressed); body painted dark green; black "Zell am See" over "Krimml" on white rectangle beneath window four; a black-outlined square with detail and lettering beneath window five. **CP**

3063 1975-86, Rhaetian (RhB) first/second class eight-wheel express train coach. Basic body composition, type SM4, same as 3062(A); painted bright red; length 460 mm.

(A) 1975-78, second and third class in Arabic numbers; doors with non-working handles; orange-yellow window frames; Medium-Arched MA4 roof (seven seams, no vents) or MA5 (seven seams, three vents); single white stripe along body beneath bases of windows; body lettering and numbers only on pinkish-red colored side corner plaque; end doors with

gates (no simulated concertina diaphragms for gangways); frame markings, if present, beneath windows two, three, four and five. May have included sheet of peel-and-stick labels, W. Gallagher comment. **120**

(B) 1979-80, same as (A), but with brass-colored working handles on doors; roof may have black shading at edges. **100**

(C) 1981-84, SM4(C) body (door hinge pinions and pinion holes relatively large, 2 mm in diameter); doors with working handles; orange stripe designating first class section; simulated concertina gangways; "nicht-raucher" beneath window one, "raucher" sign beneath window six (counting from loop end); white "Chur-St. Moritz" framed in white rectangle beneath window five; RhB at center with "AB 3063" and "44 p1. 25t" beneath it; "6.2m", "1.2m" in lower left side corner, "REV. 7.3.79" in lower right side corner; may or may not have frame markings; medium gray-painted Medium-Arched MA5 roof (seven seams, three vents), black shading at edges. **CP**

(D) 1984-86, same as (C), but with textured roof; shorter orange stripe designating first class section (only extends over two and one/half windows). **CP**

This 3060 lacks the freestanding brake hoses of current 3060s and recent 3061s; instead, its hoses are cast in relief as part of the Solid Wall railing. The triangular coupler hook and slanting uncoupler pad date it circa 1974-1977/8.

Although similar to the Swiss-inspired 3063, 3062 has an Austrian prototype used on several of that country's narrow-gauge feeder lines. Unlike 3063 and 3064, it never has lost its Accordion-gate to a walk-through bellows.

(E) 1980, similar to 3062(F), only two made. **NSS**

3063-BT0: 1980, special orange line differentiates first and second class; black decals for 1980 LGB "Big Train Operator's" Club annual car; only 75 made. **165**

3064 1977-86, second class eight-wheel coach of the Rhaetian railway (RhB) in red and white. Basically the same design as 3063; length 460 mm.
(A) 1977-78, SM4(A) body (door hinge pinions and holes small); doors with non-working handles; orange-yellow window frames; Medium-Arched MA4 roof (seven seams, no vents); body lettering and numbers only on pinkish-red lower left side corner plaque (in a relatively deep depression); gates across end doors; no simulated concertina gangways; frame markings beneath windows two, four and five (counting from loop end). **120**
(B) 1979, same as (A), but with white left side corner plaque with red lettering; more frame markings and sheet of peel-and-stick labels. **120**
(C) Same as (A), but with brass-colored working door handles; white left side corner plaque with black lettering; more frame markings. **100**
(D) 1980, same body type as (A), but Medium-Arched MA5 roof (seven seams, three vents); brass-colored working door handles; simulated concertina gangways; "2" over "nichtraucher" beneath windows one and

six; white or red "Chur Pontresina" painted beneath window two (counting from loop end); white left side corner plaque; with or without frame markings. **100**
(E) 1981-86, same as (D), but SM4(B) body (larger door hinge pinions and holes; slightly indented number-board recess). In late 1984, some of these cars were produced in beige on the white portion of body; G. Nicholson comment. **CP**

3064OE: 1986, uncatalogued; same body and roof as 3064(E), but painted blue instead of red; gold-painted graphics and markings; "Orient Express", logo, etc.; limited edition, production due in 1986. Packaged in sets of three cars; price for set. **210**

3067: 1986, Modern Rhaetian Railway (RhB) first or second class coach. Red body with yellow stripe above windows and white stripe below; Medium-Arched silver MA6 roof (ten seams running lengthwise, three small vents); special constant florescent lighting system; length 500 mm. A pre-production model has a constant brightness, fluorescent lighting system operated by lighting sockets and wire loops to connect to a locomotive. R. Enners Collection. However, production models (at least for the USA) will have current pickups in the wheels; W. Richter comment. **CP**

One of a pair of models with recent Rhaetian prototypes, 3063 and its mate have detailed lavatories with operating seat lids. Earlier versions lacked the accordion diaphragms, inoperable on the model, having Accordion-gates like 3062 instead.

Like its companion car 3063, 3064 is closely modeled on a Swiss prototype, but somewhat shortened. The main changes from version to version have been in lettering, striping, roof vents and plaques.

3068: 1986, Dining car (first pictured in 1985 German catalogue); Medium-Arched MA7 roof (similar to the type MA6 of 3067, but with one large vent added over center of dining area); kitchen compartment and dining area; same colors and lighting as 3067 (may not become available until 1987); length 550 mm.　　　　　　　　　**CP**

3070: 1981-86, DB second class eight-wheel coach (KB4i-59 class) of German Federal Railways; similar to coaches that saw service on the Mosbach/Mudau secondary railway. Dark green Simulated Metal SM5(A) body (six windows); has 48 seats with over-head luggage racks; all windows adjustable; opening sliding doors; open platforms with SA3 railings (hinged paired aisleway gates, side gates, handrails and footplates); High-Arched HA1 roof (two vents); most notable frame marking is "5 Munster"; one version produced; length 495 mm.　　　　　　　　　**CP**

3071: 1981-86, DB second class eight-wheel KBD 4i coach with baggage compartment of the German Federal Railways. A companion car to 3070, but has SM5(B) body (three windows, bifold doors, fourth window); only 24 seats with overhead luggage space; baggage compartment with paired two-section folding doors; most notable frame marking is "AW Karlsruhe"; length 495 mm; one version produced.　　　　　　　　　**CP**

3080 1981-86, Denver and Rio Grande Western Railroad (D&RGW)

Scheduled for release in 1986, with its companion diner 3068 to follow shortly, the 550 mm long 3067 is 20 percent longer than its fellow Rhaetian models, 3063 and 3064. Its engineering reflects the Richters' determination that all LGB items will be able to operate on the tightest curves, 600 mm radius. To get a feeling for its span, count the ties under the car (there are three eleven-tie pieces of foot-long #1100 track curves in a quarter circle).

Lehmann designated 3070, above, and its companion 3071 as "Supermodels" when they were introduced. Windows slide up and down; the tread plate can be lowered to horizontal, for between-car travel; a pair of end gates swings open and the platform side gates pivot upward at the car end wall, collapsing to a single line.

eight-wheel coach, which still operates daily in the summer, used between Durango and Silverton, Colorado. Bright yellow unpainted Simulated Wood SW3(A) body (nine narrow windows); Low-Arched roof with Clerestory CL4 roof (rounded down toward ends, 12 small windows on each side and black stove stacks at opposite corners); open Frame of Rods FR2 railings (two inverted "U"s with added vertical member, simulated chain); length 495 mm.

(A) Originally depicted in the German version 1981-82 catalogue without any painted details on body and an unpainted gray roof; embossed, black-painted grab-irons on ends of body; brown window frames. This car was probably not produced in this form. **NRS**

(B) 1981, simulated wooden body; red or brown window frames; black-painted sill beneath nine windows; "3080" at each end painted on sides; black band above windows with yellow "DENVER & RIO GRANDE WESTERN" over windows; embossed, black-painted grab-irons on ends of body; gold-painted railings on end sides; silver-painted roof (as depicted in the English vesions of the 1981-82 catalogue). **NRS**

(C) 1983, same as (B), but with black shading on roof edges. **CP**

(D) 1984-86, same as (B), but with dark gray roof with black shading at edges. **CP**

3080-BT0 1983, special version of 3080(C) coach for 1983 LGB "Big Train

Operator's" club annual car; same yellow body but has special black decals to commemorate meet at Strasburg, Pennsylvania; only 100 made. **155**

3081 1981-86, Denver and Rio Grande Western Railroads (D & RGW) combination coach and baggage car used between Durango and Silverton, Colorado. Same specs as 3080, but with Simulated Wood SW3(B) body (five windows, then a baggage compartment door, and then a sixth window).

(A) Same as 3080(A), but with baggage compartment; this car was probably not produced in this form. **NRS**

(B) 1981, same as 3080(B), but with baggage compartment and "3081" numbers on sides; "BAGGAGE AND EXPRESS" in small letters on panel between baggage and passenger sections. Sample car, as depicted in 1981-82 English catalogue; R. Rench comment. **NRS**

(C) 1982, same as 3080(C), but with baggage compartment. **100**

(D) 1983, same as 3080(D), but with baggage compartment. **CP**

(E) 1984-86, same as 3080(E), but with baggage compartment. **CP**

3150: 1985-86, Anniversary cars to commemorate 150 years of German railways ("Deutsche Eisenbahn"). Three versions of this four-wheel coach were produced for the 20150 set; all have red-painted Simulated Metal SM2(B) body (corner seams, one horizontal seam, unraised boards/plaques), with four orange-yellow window frames; with "3007" embossed identification number.

3071 has all the movable parts of its companion, 3070, plus a pair of double-hinged baggage compartment doors that open inward like a splitting "W".

Although shortened by three windows, 3080 is a close approximation to its western prototype, well known to American visitors to the Durango-Silverton ride up the canyon of the Las Animas River in Colorado.

(A) 1985, Furth coach. On each side of car on the panel just below the windows there is a lithographed scene of several buildings from Furth, West Germany with the name "Furth" spelled out below it; arched above the scene read the words "150 Jahre Deutsche Eisenbahn" all in gold paint. There are two white heralds with a green clover leaf just above each end of worded arch. Sold only with set 20150. **NSS**

(B) 1985, Nuremberg coach. Similar to above but depicts the city of Nuremberg, West Germany and has the "Nurnberg" name. The two heralds are two-tone black and yellow with an eagle in the center. Sold only with set 20150. **NSS**

(C) 1985-86, 150-year coach. Similar to (A) and (B), but has a painted-on, crossed-flag herald (one red and white, one blue and white) with a yellow-gold crown and wreath (wreath has yellow, blue and white in the center with a yellow bow at the bottom); flags, wreath, etc. are surrounded by the same colored tassle that is adjacent to the windows. Markings are in gold paint and include "1835" above "Deutsche" and "1985" above "Eisenbahn" to the right and left of the wreath respectively. This is the

only version of the 3150 that was sold separately yet still intended to be part of the 20150 set. **65**

3150(C) supplements the limited edition set 20150. The shield and lettering on its side panels below the windows are different from those on the two cars provided with the set.

Variation in roof shading and the addition of brass grab-irons (embossed in this photo), visible on the end panel of the car body, are the only changes in baggage car 3081 and its companion 3080 since their introduction in 1981.

Chapter VII
Goods Wagons, Flatcars, Gondolas,
Container Cars, Containers and Cabooses

A "goods wagon" or, in German, Guterwagen would be called a "freight car" by an American. Open goods wagons are used for a much wider variety of transport in the short runs common in Europe generally, short at least by continental American standards. Often, goods that in this country would be shipped in a boxcar were shipped there in open wagons, covered by a tarpaulin. Containers are increasingly common, and of course many cars are special purpose, such as the side dumping ballast wagon, hopper 4041.

4000: 1968-70, four-wheel flatcar with short bulkheads at each end; no truss rods; used by the Salzkammergut Local Railway. Unpainted black body with no painted markings; length 300 mm. Due to its extremely short production run and uninteresting appearance, few were sold in U.S. It is one of the scarcest early cars; D. Weiler comment. **300**

Gray flatcar 4001 had a ten year run, from the beginning in 1968 through 1978. It survives in its descendants, cable car 4002 and container car 4003, which have deck lugs this car lacks. The truss rods shown on this 4001(B), not on the original, were added in 1973. C. Colwell Collection.

4001: 1969-78, same basic car as 4000, but with light gray, simulated wood unpainted body; black frame; one step on each end corner.
(A) 1969-72, early chassis without truss rods; sold separately and with 20501L set. **85**
(B) 1973-78, late chassis with truss rods. **65**

One of many cars derived from the original 4000 black/4001 gray flatcars, 4002 was introduced with green cable reels in 1979; the spools were lettered in 1982, and have been yellow since 1983. The "Kabel—Union" sign changed colors in 1984. Such cars are a particularly common sight on electrified roads.

4002: 1979-86, cable wagon with two removable "Kabel-Union" cable spools (reels) as loads; similar to the type used by Messrs. Felten and Guillaume, cable manufacturers in Nuremberg. Car body is essentially the same as the 4000 or 4001, but with the addition of raised restraints for spool supports; small, upright sign on each side reading "Kabel Union"; length 300 mm.

(A) 1979-82, orange-brown body; green spools without painted markings; yellow "Kabel-Union" sign with black letters; no truss rods. **50**
(B) 1982-83, same as (A), but green spools have black and white detail markings. **55**
(C) 1983-84, medium brown body, slightly darker than (A) or (B); yellow spools with black and white detail markings. **CP**
(D) 1984-86, same as (C), but black "Kabel Union" sign with white lettering. **CP**
4002/69: 1983, same as 4003, but with 4002(A) wagon and 4069/1 container "Freizeit Hobby Spiel". May not be a Lehmann assembly. 2,000 made; B. Roth comment. See 4003F. **75**
4003: see Container Cars listed on page 67.

4010 shares with nine other cars the honor of illustration in the very first Lehmann catalogue, and has been available over the years in several greens and browns. Originally brown (companion 4011 was green), the latest version is painted green.

4010: 1968-86, black chassis low-sided gondola used in large quantities by all European railway companies. Four-wheel, with simulated wood exterior and inside flooring; length 300 mm.
(A) 1968-74, unpainted straw brown body; F1 frame without truss rods; no slots in center of gondola sides and ends; no painted markings or detail on body or frame. **150**
(B) 1971-74, same as (A), but reportedly unpainted medium green; comment requested. Also exists with truss rods; J. Barton comment. **175**
(C) 1976-78, same as (A), but with unpainted medium brown body; black F2 frame with truss rods; slots in center of gondola sides only; no end slots; no markings. Sold with set 20501JR. **35**
(D) 1973-83, same as (B), but with Type 1 frame markings; slots both in center of sides and ends. **26**
(E) 1983, same as (B), but has white markings which include "4010 x 05" on the left-hand side of center gondola side panels; white and black-painted side grate screens. **100**
(F) 1983-86, green-painted body exterior with same markings as (E); light blue-gray, whitish-green or gray-painted interior; Type 1 frame markings. **CP**

Take a 4010 body, paint it orange and add a pyramidal six-door lid, and you have the "Hilfswagen" or "help-car" with the reassigned number 4011. The superstructure is easily removable. Such a car would be a standard component of a work train.

4010FO: 1984, same simulated wood exterior and interior flooring body and color as 4010(B) or (C), but with white "FO" (Furka-Oberalp), "KK1 4606" and "6.0m" on center of gondola sides; "14,5m" and "10t/6600Kg" on right-hand gondola side panel. Sold separately and with 20512 and/or 20515 train set.   **38**

4011: 1968-74, four-wheel, low-sided gondola similar to 4010, but with dark green unpainted body; no markings on body or frame.   **175**

4011: 1979-86, hinged-hatch wagon K "Hilfswagen" of the OEG; auxiliary wagon for transporting bulk goods sensitive to moisture and for railroad company's own maintenance and auxillary materials; all six hatches can be opened independently; main body same as 4010 but orange-painted body with black markings; Type 1 or 2 frame markings; length 300 mm.

(A) 1979, "Hilfswagen" on side beneath middle hatch; "OEG" over "696" on end body panel; may be the prototype.   **NRS**

(B) 1979-86, "Hilfswagen" on side beneath right hatch between fourth and fifth stanchion supports; "OEG" at the side of "4011" between second and third stanchion supports; red and white hazard markings at corners.   **CP**

4011BTO: 1982, LGB Model Railroad "Big Train Operator's" Club Fourth Annual convention car; repainted bright red with white silk-screened lettering on doors to commemorate convention and Trainland at Coleman's Nursery in Portsmouth, Virginia. Type 1 frame markings.   **85**

4020: 1968-74, four-wheel, high-sided gondola Ow. Opening side doors with lift-latch for lock; simulated wooden grain inside and out; unpainted straw brown body; black grab-rails on ends; no markings on body or frame; length 300 mm.   **200**

4021: 1968-86, same basic car as 4020, but in green or darker brown than 4020.

(A) 1968-74, unpainted medium green body without markings; no markings on frame.   **160**

Although 4020, discontinued in 1974, was always brown, its companion car 4021, like 4010, has been various colors, including two browns, two greens, and — for Primus — both blue and yellow. This type of car is often used in Europe as a general freight car, transporting a much wider variety of goods, often under tarpaulin, than its American equivalents.

(B) 1972-76, unpainted darker green body; no markings on frame.   **135**

(C) 1975-78, unpainted medium green body; white "LGB", "Ow" and "4021" on lower half of first body panel; no frame markings.   **65**

(D) 1979-80, unpainted darker green body than (C) with black chalkboard in lower portion of first body panel, black-painted frame on grate on second body panel; no frame markings. Also came painted; C. Colwell comment.
                                                                         30

(E) 1981-83, similar to (C), but with painted body and Type 1 frame markings.   **30**

(F) 1983, same as (D), but with gondola interior painted light gray; Type 1 or 2 frame markings.   **40**

(G) 1983-84, medium brown-painted body; light gray-painted interior; white lettering, numerals.   **CP**

(H) 1985-86, similar to (G), but with darker brown-painted body.   **CP**

To the right of the low-sided, brown 4010 ("Niederbordwagen") is a green 4011. Below them is the high-sided ("Hochbordwagen") brown 4020, beside a green 4021; this 4021 and the one below it date from the 1980s, differing from that brown 4021(G) in color and from each other in the green interior of (D) and the gray interior of (E). Lettering and color date the 4061 at lower left between 1974 and 1976. A. Rudman Collection.

The two hoppers 4041(B) and 4041G, both out of production, are based on prototypes in the Upper Rhine Railway Company ("Oberrheinische-Eisenbahn-Gesellschaft"). Log car 4066(B), 1974-1978, can be identified by lettering and the appearance of the logs. A. Rudman Collection.

(I) 1979-80, unpainted yellow body, same as (D), but has Type 1 frame markings; made for Primus. **NRS**

(J) 1979-80, unpainted blue body, same as 4021(A) or (B), came with Primus starter set 8000; made for Primus. **NRS**

4041: 1971-86, OEG four-wheel ballast hopper car, based on the 1200 built in 1925 by the H. Fuchs Coach Works in Heidelberg that had a carrying capacity of 15,000 kg. Manually-operated chute doors on sides to empty loads; came with bag of ballast (multi-colored chopped-up bits of plastic in a plastic bag); FA1 railing (Frame of Angle iron, with off-center vertical and

incomplete horizontal member), the only asymmetrical railing, unique to this car; length 300 mm. The bits of plastic "ballast," the raw pellets that LGB cars are made of, did not come with early cars; B. Roth comment.

(A) 1971-73, semi-glossy, unpainted red hopper portion of car (red color may fade to pinkish-red on some pieces), black simulated wood floor, four steps near each corner of sides; FA1(A) railing (Frame of Angle iron, asymmetrical, with brake pipes and hose cast in plane of railing); white detail markings; black or red chute, hand-crank wheels and supports; "O.E.G." on center panel in oval-shaped letters; "OEG" and "1200" more

The railing of 4041, with its asymmetrical arrangement, is specific to this car. Late versions have the free-standing brake hose; earlier ones had a brake hose cast in the plane of the railing. Older cars were cranberry or red, with a very early gray version 4041G. The hopper doors operate, and can dump plastic pellets to trackside.

The prototype model 4059 lacks the extensive lettering and large railing plaque of the production model. In this picture, the rear apron is up, in traveling position, while the front apron is down, in loading position: Cars endload, driving on and off the length of the train. Through mountain tunnels, passengers usually stay with the cars.

robust than in subsequent versions; white heat-stamped markings on small dispatch boards on lower left supports of hopper body; white heat-stamped frame markings directly above chutes. **145**

(B) 1974-78, same as (A), but with bright, glossy red-painted hopper. **115**

(C) 1979-82, similar to (B), but with thinner, more delicately defined frame markings; "OEG" and "1200" on center panel of hopper; "OEG" on hopper panel is comprised of rounded rather than oval letters; no working present on small display boards at lower left aspect of hopper body. **70**

(D) 1980, uncatalogued; similar to (C), but with dull-finished, dark cranberry red-painted hopper body; FA1(B) railing (heavier Angle iron, right brake pipe and hose separate castings, at right angle to plane of railing). **100**

(E) 1980-81, uncatalogued; similar to (D), but with semi-glossy, dark cranberry red-painted hopper body. **100**

(F) 1983-86, unpainted orange hopper body with simulated wooden base, black markings; orange chute, hand-cranks, wheels and supports; black "OEG/737" instead of "1200"; four steps (half size of earlier ones); red and white hazard markings on side corners; black dispatch board with white information on chute supports. **CP**

4041G: 1971-74, OEG four-wheel ballast hopper car; similar to 4041(A), but with light gray-colored body. Also produced for Primus; B. Cage and J. Hylva comments. Quite scarce; D. Weiler comment. **275**

4042: Matra-Frankfurt crane car. See service wagon section on page 83.

The five cars pictured here represent four versions of 4060, varying in color, road name and lettering: top left, 4060(F); top right, 4060(D) or (E) (to tell which you would check the color of the undercarriage supports); middle left, 4060(B), which lacks the raised lugs to hold containers in place on the deck; middle right and bottom, 4060(G) unloaded and with load. Note that some of the arch bar truck frames are the recent gray, others black. A. Rudman Collection.

The low-sided gondola 4061 has gone through several shades of brown and red, atop what is basically a black 4060 flatcar. The truss rods, on the prototype, were meant to keep the car's center from sagging under heavy loads, as it aged. If over tightened, to correct sag, they sometimes bowed the center upwards.

4059: 1985, automobile transport flatcar with two late model Mercedes 150 sedans. This is basically an eight-wheel flatcar similar to the 4060 painted black; length 415 mm. Markings: Between first and second stake pockets at left, "Waggon Fabrik" over "1985 14059" over "Talbot" all in an oval, with "6300kg" boxed to the right; between second and third pockets, "LuP 9,3m"; between third and fourth pockets, "LGB"; between fourth and fifth pockets, "4059" (this and the preceding are the most prominent body markings); between fifth and sixth, "Rev 07 90" boxed; to right of sixth pocket, "5.9m" between arrows; plus "LGB Expresss" in yellow on black background in right-hand guardrails. Although the 1985 catalogue showed this car with gray guardrails, it was produced with yellow/orange ones. The two oval-shaped guardrails per side fit into the first and third and the fifth and seventh stanchion pockets. There is one yellow and black striped flip-up type loading gate at each end for securing as well as allowing automobiles to be loaded or unloaded from the bed. A raised ramp covering the center section of the flat bed has depressions for holding automobile wheels in place. The die-cast automobiles are not made by Lehmann; B. Rench and V. Winn comments. **CP**

4060: 1971-86, eight-wheel flatcar (platform wagon) with insertable stanchions; has seven stanchion pockets per side; arch bar trucks; length 415 mm.
(A) 1971-72, unpainted light straw brown color simulated wood bed and four truss rod supports; no numbers or lettering; black plastic stanchions; bed lacks the raised tabs found on subsequent versions for securing 4069/1 containers. **NRS**
(B) 1973-76, same as (A), but with white "4060" added to each side of bed between fifth and sixth stanchion pockets. **75**

(C) 1977, unpainted orange-brown bed and undercarriage supports; black plastic stanchions; bed has eight raised tabs for securing 4069/1 containers; "4060" on each side between fifth and sixth stanchion pockets; same car as 4069(A). **90**
(D) 1978-79, same as (C), but with "CAPY 20050" between second and third stanchion pockets, "S.P." placed between third and fourth stanchion pockets, "4060" between fourth and fifth stanchion pockets, "LT WT 14500" between fifth and sixth stanchion pockets, "RPKD OYO" above "38 11 20 39" between sixth and seventh stanchion pockets. **45**
(E) 1980-82, same as (D), but with black undercarriage supports. **36**
(F) 1983-84, medium brown-painted flat bed with black undercarriage supports; "CAPY 20050" between second and third stanchion pocket, "D&RGW" between fourth and fifth stanchion pockets, "LT WT 11500" between fifth and sixth stanchion pockets, "ALA-6.13" over "BLT-5.88" between sixth and seventh stanchion pockets. **38**
(G) 1984, uncatalogued; similar to (F), but with flat bed painted flat black over orange-brown plastic; same bed markings as (F). **40**
(H) 1985-86, similar to (F), but bed is unpainted orange-brown. **CP**

4061: 1971-86, low-sided gondola car as used on the Hartsfeld Railway and many U.S. lines. Brakeman's platform with hand brake wheel; no railing; basically the same eight-wheel flatcar as 4060, but black; bed has a four-sided gondola secured by stanchions fitting into pockets; length 415 mm.
(A) 1971-73, no markings or lettering on bed of gondola; no raised tabs for securing 4069/1 containers; black, unpainted bed; reddish-pink, unpainted gondola without embossed details such as rivet heads on stanchions, rope eyelets or "4061" as seen on more recent models. May be prototype; J. Hylva comment. **NRS**

Unfamiliar to American eyes are the brakeman's hut and heavy truss beam of open goods wagon 4062, a high-sided gondola first modeled in 1973. Changes include changes in color toward this darker, more orange-brown, the freestanding brake hose replacing the one cast in relief on the hut and, as so often, increased lettering.

(B) 1974-76, same as (A), but with the following white markings: "CAPY 40 000" above "WT l5 900K 2 24" between second and third stanchion pockets, "S P" (spaced apart and without periods) between third and fourth stanchions pockets, "4061" ("4" is open at top) between fourth and fifth stanchion pockets, "IL 26" (spaced apart) above "CU FT 369" between fifth and sixth stanchion pockets; embossed details, "LGB" logo and "4061" on reddish-pink gondola sides.   75

(C) 1976-78, similar to (B), but with unpainted medium brown gondola.   100

(D) 1976-?, similar to (B), but with unpainted dark green gondola. J. Hylva Collection.   500

(E) 1977-81, same as (B), but with raised tabs for securing 4069/1 containers of bed; gondola sides red-painted over brown plastic; markings include "S.P." between third and fourth stanchion pockets, "4061" (4 is closed at top) between fourth and fifth stanchion pockets, markings between second and third stanchion pockets same as (B) but reduced in size, "IL 26" (spaced apart) above "CU PT 269" between sixth and seventh stanchion pockets, additional markings "RPKD MINA" over "UP 1832" between sixth and seventh stanchion pockets.   65

(F) 1982, same as (E), but with flat black-painted bed.   75

(G) 1983-86, similar to (E), but with bed painted flat black; gondola same red color as (E) or slightly darker; notches to clear container securing tabs; most markings are reduced in size as compared to (E) and differ as follows: "D&RGW" between third and fourth stanchion pockets, "CAPY 40000" (no space between second and third zeroes) above "WT 13900 ALA 12", "ALA-5.12" above "BLT-8.92" between sixth and seventh stanchion pockets.   CP

4062: 1973-86, eight-wheel, high sided gondola (00m/s class) used by the Pinzgau Local Railway. Eight opening doors on sides of body and a brakeman's cab with opening doors; FA3 railing (Frame of Angle iron, half in relief); arch bar trucks; length 430 mm.

(A) 1973-74, light straw brown body without markings; FA3(A) railing (brakeman's cab has embossed brake hose); no markings on frame. May be prototype; J. Hylva comment.   NRS

(B) 1974-75, similar to (A), but with white, heat-stamped markings limited to the first two body panels adjacent to the brakeman's platform.   85

(C) 1975-81, orange-brown body, white heat-stamped markings on first two body panels adjacent to brakeman's platform.   68

(D) 1982-83, same as (C), but with silk-screened markings which include "4062LGB" over vent gate at center, side of car body; FA3(B) railing (freestanding right-hand brake pipe and hose, not embossed on cab).   45

(E) 1984-86, same as (C), but with silk-screened frame markings spaced at eight intervals; no embossed brake hose on brakeman's cab.   CP

4065: 1971-86, short "bobber" four-wheel caboose of the Denver Rio Grande Western narrow gauge railway; brakeman's platforms at each end; FR1 railings (open Frame of Rods, two inverted "U"s joined by a chain); roof with stove smokestack; centered cupola with roof vent; produced with 3000/1 spoked wheels; has buffers, unlike most American equipment; length 300 mm.

(A) 1971-75, unpainted pinkish-red body without any markings; embossed black-painted grab-irons on body.   135

(B) 1973-75, same as (A), but with white "4065" on lower center of each side.   100

(C) 1974-78, same as (A), but with white "4065" on lower center of each side, "Rio Grande" between side windows of body.   100

(D) 1978-79, uncatalogued; pinkish-red body; embossed black-painted grab-irons; round-shaped, white logo placed between "Rio Grande" and "4065" comprised of "Rio Grande", "Royal Gorge", "Moffat Tunnel" and "Scenic Line of The World".   NRS

(E) 1979-82, same as (D), but with brownish-red-painted body and cupola; white "WT 20300" above "ALA 6-32" added to lower right corner of body. On some pieces the cupola and body color were of a slightly different hue.   55

(F) 1982-86, same as (E), but with brass wire grab-irons on body. Some cars may have had the spaces between wooden slats on body and cupola painted white; M. Richter comment.   CP

4065BTO: 1985, produced for LGB Model RR Club as 1985 annual car; brownish-red painted body has a series of decals to commemorate the event held at Portsmouth Virginia. Cars were prepared by Al Lentz.   150

4065FL: 1982, similar to 4065(E), but with Florsheim decal over body markings.   65

4066: 1973-86, lumber car with stanchions with chains and load of five logs; underside detailed with brake cylinder, piping and steps; brakeman's wheel on side; has buffers, unlike most American equipment; length 410 mm. The major variations have more to do with the logs than the car itself.

(A) 1973-74, green bed with black stanchions; no white markings on car; very light plastic logs are of varied diameter with thick bark and are quite realistic looking.   80

(B) 1974-78, same as (A), but with the white "N.W.L. Co." above "4066" at center side edge of bed; logs are more uniform in shape and size.   50

(C) 1979-84, same as (A), but with white "N.W.L. Co." above "4066" at center side edge of flat bed; logs appearing more like telephone posts; bark is weakly simulated.   35

(D) 1984-86, similar to (C), but with the following markings on chassis sides: "Vorsichtig rangieren", "Hardy-Bremse Drehzapf. Abst. 5,8m", "Lup 9,25m", "LGB/4066", "8, 35mm", "9500 kg", "REV09.12.85".   CP

4073: 1985-86, eight-wheel, high-sided gondola of the narrow gauge U.S. rail lines, unpainted maroon-brown with white markings and logos of the Denver and Rio Grande Western Railroad (prototype depicted in 1985-86

The cabooses can be dated 1973 left, and 1979-1982, right, by color, uncoupling pads, lettering and the absence of brass grab-irons. A. Rudman Collection.

Log car 4066 has varied little since its introduction in 1973, mostly in lettering. But the logs have changed several times, now approximating telephone poles more nearly than the richly textured bark of the earliest version.

catalogue is painted dark brown). Body is composed of simulated wooden plank sides with ten stanchions on each side for support. (This car is not another variation of the 4060 flatcar.) The grab-irons are cast separately in black plastic and are attached to side and ends; markings (all painted in white) include a round-shaped logo containing the words "D&RGWRR", "ROYAL GORGE ROUTE" and "SCENIC LINE" between the first and second stanchions. "D&RGW 1646" is painted on the sides of the flat bed between the first and fourth stanchions, "1646" is on the second side plank from the top between the fifth and sixth stanchions, "CAPY 50000 LBS." is on the same plank between the sixth and eighth stanchions and "Wt. 20400" above "SAL 10-26" are on the bottom side planks between the seventh and eighth stanchions; "LENGTH INSIDE 30 FT 10 IN" above "WIDTH INSIDE 6 FT 11 IN" above "HEIGHT INSIDE 4 FT 2 IN" are on the bed between the seventh and ninth stanchions; "BUILT 10-82" is on the bed between the ninth and tenth stanchions; "D&RGW" above "1646" is at the upper right-hand corner of each end.   **CP**

CONTAINER CARS

4003: 1983-86, four-wheel container car with single six meter container; same basic car as the 4002 but produced in black plastic and painted flat black; first sold with 4069/1 (G) container but has also been seen with other versions; length 300 mm. Price includes car with container.   **CP**

4003A: 1985, uncatalogued; Abele Company container car; on standard 4003 flatcar with 4069/1A container painted silver with black markings; sold only with set 20531A.   **NSS**

4003B: 1985, uncatalogued; Breuninger Company container car; on standard 4003 flatcar with 4069/1B container painted brown (same brown as 4003SB) with gold markings; sold only with set 20531B.   **125**

4003BTO: 1984, annual car for 1984 LGB Model Railroader Club Big Train Operator's Convention. Same basic bed as 4003 flatcar; less than 60 made.
(A) With 4069/1BTO(A) container; only six made.   **150**
(B) With 4069/1BTO(B) container; only about 50 made.   **75**

4003CS: 1985, uncatalogued; Capri-Sonne container car; on standard 4003 flatcar with 4069/1CS container painted blue with white and orange lettering; sold only with set 20531CS.   **125**

4003D: 1984, uncatalogued; white DHS container car; same as 4003 with 4069/1D white container with red, black and green markings; sold with set 20514 and boxed separately; container held on to black chassis with doubled rubber band from buffer to buffer; black "SPIEL" and "HOBBY" between pairs of orange and green stripes. 800 made.   **75**

4003DV: 1985, uncatalogued; Dauth Company container car; on standard 4003 flatcar with 4069/1DV container painted silver with black markings; sold only with set 20531DV.   **NSS**

4003F: 1982, uncatalogued; Freizeit Hobby Spiel (FHS) container car comprised of a 4002 orange-brown colored flatcar and 4069/1F white container with red, blue and orange markings; erroneously dubbed 4002/69 by collectors; available only with set 20502.   **NSS**

4003K: 1985, uncatalogued; Kurtz container car, on standard 4003 flatcar with 4069/1K container painted yellow with black markings; sold only with set 20531K.   **NSS**

4003KT: 1985, uncatalogued; Kenner Trinken Wurtemberger container car on standard 4003 flatcar with 4069/1KT silver-painted container with black, red and brown markings; sold only with set 20531KT.   **125**

4003L: 1985, uncatalogued Lindau container car on standard 4003 flatcar with 4069/IL container painted silver with black markings; sold only with set 20531L.   **NSS**

Issued in a much darker brown than its original catalogue photograph, 4073 continues Lehmann's expansion of its line of American prototype models. The trucks of this entirely newly designed body are arch bar, a type characteristic of American freight cars until the development of roller bearings and modern high speed, high capacity trucks.

4003, the four-wheel single-container car, was introduced in 1983, and has since been issued with a large variety of specially decorated containers in limited edition sets. It is basically the same car as 4002, with cable load, or 4000 and 4001, discontinued flatcars. A. Rudman Collection.

4003MC: 1985, uncatalogued; Modellbahn-Center (MC) container car on standard 4003 flatcar with 4069/1MC container; sold only with set 20531MC.   125

4003NF: 1985, Nurnberg Furth 150 Anniversary car, same color as 4003RZ container car, but with red and white 150 Nurnberg Furth Anniversary decal instead of LGB logo; with container 4069/1NF; car and container.   65

4003P: 1985, uncatalogued; Panne Company container car on standard 4003 flatcar with 4069/1P container painted silver with black markings; sold only with set 20531P.   NSS

4003PV: 1984, uncatalogued; "Commander Rom" container car on standard 4003 flatcar with 4069/1PV dark blue container; sold only with Philips Video set 380.7030.   NSS

4003RZ: 1983-84, uncatalogued; LGB "der Rot Zug" (The Red Train) container car with 4003 flatcar and 4069/1RZ(A) red, white and green container; sold only with set 20401RZ.   NSS

4003S: 1985, uncatalogued; Schinacher Company container car; on standard 4003 flatcar with 4069/1S container painted silver with black markings; sold only with set 20531S.   NSS

4003SB: 1984, uncatalogued; Schmidt Bakery container car, on standard 4003 flatcar with 4069/1SB container painted chocolate brown with white and red markings; sold only with set 20526.   NSS

4003SF: 1985, uncatalogued; Schnabel Company container car, on standard 4003 flatcar with 4069/1SF container car painted silver with black markings; sold only with set 20531SF.   NSS

4003SR: 1984, uncatalogued; Spielzeug Ring container car, on standard 4003 flatcar with 4069/1SF white container with green and yellow markings; sold separately. 1,000 made; B. Roth comment.   75

4003TS: 1985, uncatalogued; Sindel Company container car, on standard 4003 flatcar with 4069/1TS container painted silver with black markings; sold only with set 20531TS   NSS

4003Z: 1985, uncatalogued; Zinthafner Company container car, on standard 4003 flatcar with 4069/1Z container painted silver with black markings; sold only with set 20531Z.   NSS

4069: 1977-86, eight-wheel flatcar with two four-wheel trucks; two removable 4069/1 containers; bed has eight raised tabs to secure the containers; length 415 mm. Listed prices are for flatcar without containers; for complete pricing values combine price of flatcar with price of corresponding 4069/1 containers. The earliest catalogue photograph shows 4060(B) flatcar with 4069/1(A) containers; however the first issue was actually the 4060(C) flatcar. Prices are for flatcar with containers.

(A) 1977-78, orange-brown bed; with "4060" between fifth and sixth stanchion pockets, same flatcar as 4060(C); this is the earliest version sold and usually had 4069/1(A) container. Price for car and containers.   135
(B) 1978-80, unpainted black bed; with "4069" between fifth and sixth stanchion pockets, usually with 4069/1(B) containers.   70
(C) 1980, same as (B), but with 4069/1(C) containers.   68
(D) 1980, same as (B), but with 4069/1(D) containers.   100

(E) 1980-81, same as (B), but with "4069" between fourth and fifth stanchion pockets, "S.P." between third and fourth stanchion pockets, "CAPY 40000" over "WT 13 900K 224" between second and third stanchion pockets, "IL 26" over "CU FT 269" between fifth and sixth stanchion pockets, "RPKD MINA" over "UP 1732" between sixth and seventh stanchion pockets; usually with 4069/1(C) or (E) containers.   38
(F) 1983-86, European version with bed either unpainted black or painted flat black; "4069" between fourth and fifth stanchion pockets, "LGB" between third and fourth stanchion pockets, "Wagonfabrik Talbot 1965 4069" inside an oval next to "9600kg" between first and second stanchion pockets, "LuP 9,3m" between second and third stanchion pockets, "REV 03 85" between fifth and sixth stanchion pockets, "5,9m" between sixth and seventh stancion pockets; packaged with 4069/1(E) or (F) or 4069/1RZ(B) containers.   CP

CONTAINERS

4069/1: 1977-86, models of six meter transport containers for simplified freight handling for use by rail, road or sea. Roof pins for securing stacking; doors can be opened; length 170 mm. Sold separately in sets of two or with a 4003 single container car or a 4069 double container car.

(A) 1977-78, white container with large green and yellow peel-and-stick "LGB" logo on each side. Price for two containers and 4069(A) container car.   135
(B) 1978-80, white container with smaller red and yellow logo combined with horizontal stripe just below midline on each side of container; red color of stripe touches outside red outline of logo; "LGB" over "Ht" at top of sixth side panel, "00" above "6 252" at top of seventh panel, "5069" above "2360kg" at top of eighth panel, "Eigegewicht" divided between tops of sixth and seventh panels, two solid black rectangles at bottom of sixth panel; "Gewahr GW", "Behalter 17.7.7", "Anstrich Sp. H.", "20.7.7" and cross-hatching all at the bottom of the eighth panel. Container doors have the following markings: the top of the left door has "LGB" logo; the top of the right door has "LGB 00 5069", "Groptes", "Gesamtgew. 20320 kg" and "Eigengew. 2360 kg". Price for pair only.   45
(C) 1980-81, same as (B), but with light gray container. Price for pair only.   35
(D) 1980-81, uncatalogued; same as (C), but with green and yellow "LGB" logo and stripe. Price for pair only.   65
(E) 1981-82, same as (C), but markings differ as follows: "Eigengewicht" and "Ht 6 252" reduced in size and limited to the top of the sixth panel, "5069" and "2360 kg" at top of seventh panel, "Zum Aw" above "12.83 bis 12.85" at bottom of fifth panel; "Gewahrl." with Thyssen logo above "Container 12.81" at bottom of seventh panel. More cross-hatching at bottom of eighth panel than in (C), with Thyssen logo; "12.80", "05.81", "12.81" vertically with Thyssen logo; "12.90", "05.81", "12.81" and vertically situated "Besichtigungen". The left door has a solid black rectangle added to the lower portion, the right door is much the same as (C), but markings are reduced in size with "OFFNEN","OUVRIR", "ABRIR" and "APRIRE" added near the latch. Price for pair only.   35
(F) 1982-86, same as (E), but red color of stripe does not touch red outline of "LGB" logo and the symbol "R" for registered trademark is at the top right of the "LGB" logo. Price for pair only.   CP
(G) 1984, white container with blue horizontal stipe on sides; "VEREIN-SUND WESTBANK HAMBURG" in darker blue letters; sold with 4003 container car; price for both.   45
(H) 1985, uncatalogued; similar to (G), but with a red and yellow stripe; sold with 4003 container car; price for both.   45

4069/1A: 1985, uncatalogued; Abele Company container commissioned by same company of Aalen, West Germany; container is painted silver with "ABELE" in heavy black lettering, with Vedes logo to its left and "SPIEL & FREIZEIT" to its right, also in black; sold with 4003A container car, only with set 20531A.   NSS

4069/1B: 1985, uncatalogued; Breuninger Company container commissioned by same company of Stuttgart, West Germany; container is painted chocolate brown with "BREUNINGER" in large yellow letters above "Stuttgart ... & Spielwaren", also in yellow; sold only with 4003B container car in set 20531B.   NSS

4069/1BTO: 1984, uncatalogued; LGB Model Railroad Club 1984 National Convention Car; two versions made by Al Lentz; price is for container and 4003 container car.

(A) 1984, container has Chicago freight logo and a pronouncement of the 1984 LGB Model RR Club at the "Chateau Louise". Only six of these pieces were made due to the closing of that hotel just prior to the convention. Chateau Louise was the original site picked by the Chicago Chapter; however due to the hotel's financial problems the site was changed to the Clock Tower Inn at Rockford, Illinois. The Chateau Louise containers were made prior to cancellation notice. The meeting was relocated at the "Clock Tower" hotel. Entire side of container done with a peel-and-stick decal. Upper left side says "Port of Chicago", center "1984", upper right "Chateau Louise". Across middle in black letters on blue stripe. "Big Train Operator's"; bottom left is LGB logo. Bottom center and right, "6th Annual Convention". **150**

(B) 1984, very similar to (A), but with wording to commemorate 1984 LGB Model Railroad Club Convention at Clock Tower Inn in Rockford, Illinois (the location of the actual convention); about 50 cars made. **75**

4069/1CS: 1985, uncatalogued; Capri-Sonne container painted royal blue with "Capri-Sonne" in white and orange on each side above the words "Oberall. Fruchtig Kuhl und fruchtig prall." in white; sold only with 4003CS container car in set 20531CS. **125**

4069/1D: 1984, uncatalogued; DHS white container with red, green and white diagonal stripe on sides and "Spiel and Hobby" as part of stripe; figure of teddy bear is on the doors; sold only with 4003 container car in set 20514 or separately as 4003D car. Price for container and car. **75**

4069/1DV: 1985, uncatalogued; Dauth Company container commissioned by same company of Tubingen, West Germany (Dauth is part of the Vedes chain of stores); container is painted silver with "Vedes...Fachgeschaft" logo to the right of the Dauth logo on each side; the Dauth logo is a rectangle with the words "Spiel & Freizeit" above "Dauth" (with a rocking horse to its left) above "Tubingen" inside and the words "...immer ein guter Rot mehr" outside and just above the rectangle, all in black printing; sold only with 4003DV container car in set 20531DV. **NSS**

4069/1F: 1982, uncatalogued; FHS container, white with two, two-tone, non-intersecting stripes of red and blue, each of which forms a right angle but does not run parallel to the edges of the container. Beneath the left stripe are the words "Freizeit Hobby Spiel" in black. The right stripe is interrupted by a square logo with rounded corners outlined in blue with an orange-colored line-drawn clown's head inside; sold only with 4003F container car in set 20502. **NSS**

4069/1K: 1985, uncatalogued; Kurtz Company container, yellow-painted container with black-lettered "Spielwaren Kurtz" with a toy soldier on horseback logo; other black lettering includes the words "Stuttgart. Leonberg. Kirshheim/Teck"; sold only with 4003K container car in set 20531K. **NSS**

4069/1KT: 1985, uncatalogued; Kenner Trinken Wurtemberger container; painted silver with company logo depicting a man sipping a glass of wine in black and red and the company's coat of arms in black, red and brown, with "Genossenschaftskellerei" above it and the words "Heilbronn-Erlenbach-Weinsberge G." below it; sold only with 4003KT container car in set 20531KT. **125**

4069/1L: 1985, uncatalogued; Lindau Container commissioned by the Thommes Company, Lindau, West Germany; container is painted silver with entrance to the Lindau harbor depicted in black and "Lindau" to its right; sold only with 4003L container car in set 20531L. **NSS**

4069/1MC: 1985, uncatalogued; Modellbahn-Center (MC) container commissioned by Modelleisenbahn Center Schuler, Stuttgart, West Germany; container is painted royal blue with red "MC" logo and the words "Modellbahn-Center" above "Container-Service" also in red; sold only with 4003MC container car in set 20531MC. **125**

4069/1P: 1985, uncatalogued; Panne Company container commissioned by Panne, Reutlingen, West Germany; container is painted silver with the Panne logo and name in black; the words "Triebwagons" and "Modellbahn-station" are adjacent to logo also in black print; sold only with 4003P container car in set 20531P. **NSS**

4069/1PV: 1984, uncatalogued; Philips Video dark blue-painted container with white, light blue and pink-colored "Commander Rom" video figure emitting an electrical flash from his left hand with the words "VIDEO-SPIELE VON PHILIPS" inside it; small red and white computerized video bodies and figures cover most of the dark blue background; sold only on 4003PV container car with 380.7030 train set. **NSS**

4069/1RZ: 1983-85, uncatalogued; Der Rot Zug (the Red Train) container made as part of a promotional set and as a separate item for the Lehmann Company; two versions:

(A) 1983-84, painted cranberry red or bright red, glossy or at least semi-gloss finish; with a green and white horizontal stripe (green center stripe with white borders) just above the midline on each side of the container; a white and red circle with a red and white LGB logo in its center interrupts the stripe on the left side; sold only with 4003RZ container car in set 20401RZ. **NSS**

Container wagons are the heart of much modern freight traffic. Like the 4060 flatcars on which it is based, the car of 4069 varies primarily in lettering. In addition, a variety (thirty have been listed) of containers have accompanied it, especially in limited edition sets.

A collection of special livery cars prepared for participants in the annual conventions of the American LGB Club, publisher of the "B.T.O. Newsletter." "B.T.O." stands for "Big Train Operator's." The club was organized by Al Lentz, who originated the idea of these post-factory, special occasion liveries. Since typically no more than 100 of each car were run, they are rare. Top, 4040BTO (75 issued) and 4011BTO; second rank, 4070 (100); third rank, 4003BTO (about 50, but only six for Chateau Louise because of a site change) and 3063 (75); bottom, 4065BTO and 3080BTO (100). Not shown: 4047(E). Reader comments requested on the number of 4011BTO and 4065BTO.

(B) 1985, very similar to above, but red color is slightly brighter yet has a flat finish; green and white stripes and markings are somewhat translucent due to a lighter coat of paint; sold in pairs with 4069(D) container car and may have also been sold with 4003. **CP**

4069/1S: 1985, uncatalogued; Schinacher Company container commissioned by Schinacher, Friedrichshafen, West Germany; container is painted silver and has a black rectangle with "Schinacher" in silver letters inside it; to the right of rectangle are the words "SPIEL & FREIZEIT" in black; sold only with 4003S container car in set 20531S. **NSS**

4069/1SB: 1984, uncatalogued; Schmidt Bakery, chocolate brown-painted container with red and white Schmidt Bakery logo on the right side of container; white "hmm...Schmidt-Lebkuchen aus Nurnberg" next to logo; sold with 4003 container car in set 20526. **NSS**

4069/1SF: 1985, uncatalogued; Schnabel Company container car commissioned by Schnabel, Schwabisch-Gmund, West Germany; container is painted silver and has the "Schnabel" logo with a teddy bear head and the words "Spiel & Freizeit" above it, also has the address "Schwab. Gmund Ledergasse 63-65" to the right of logo, all in black print; sold only with 4003SF in set 20531SF. **NSS**

4069/1SR: 1984, uncatalogued; Spielzeug Ding white container with yellow and green horizontal stripes around middle of body; green "DER SPIELZEUG DING" above stripes, "DAS TOLLE DING" below stripes. Price with 4003SR container car. **75**

4069/1TS: 1985, uncatalogued; Sindel Company container commissioned by Sindel, Ulm, West Germany; container is painted silver with "TECHNIC SINDEL" across top of each side with "Donaustrasse 2 Ulm" below and figure of a model airplane, remote control car, model boat, remote control radio and steam locomotive along lower portion of each side, all in black; sold only with 4003TS container car in set 20531TS. **NSS**

4069/1Z: 1985, uncatalogued; Zinthafner Company container commissioned by Zinthafner, Ludwigsburg, West Germany; container is painted silver with company logo and the words "Spiel & Freizeit Zinthafner" all in black; sold only with 4003Z container car in set 20531Z. **NSS**

Chapter VIII
Covered Goods Wagons and Refrigerator Cars

Covered goods wagons, or closed freight cars, are the staple in any general purpose railroad's rolling stock. They come in various lengths. Short runs have encouraged European lines to use some shorter wagons than those common in America, where 32-foot boxcars were once common and 40-foot cars are still fairly standard, in contrast to the 22-foot cars of European narrow gauge lines. On both continents, more modern cars are longer.

Lehmann's many 300 mm long freight cars (representing 22-foot prototypes) are closely related in design, and sometimes (e.g. 4032L, 4034), as with passenger cars 3000/3006, a run has been made with a body embossed with a different number from the official one under which the car is catalogued, made, packaged and sold.

All 300 mm boxcars with platforms have SW1 railings (Solid Wall with triangular side gates) if produced through 1978, and FA4 railings (open Frame of Angle iron, no side gates) if produced from 1981-1985. 300 mm boxcars produced in 1979-1980 have SA1 railings (Solid wall with Accordion-gated aisleway, triangular side gates).

4029: 1971-74, four-wheel boxcar used by most railway companies. Medium-Arched roof, filigree roof supports; unpainted light brown body without markings; no frame markings; sliding doors open, early versions have simulated door on body end at brakeman's platform; two vents with horizontal grills on each side of body near roof line; embossed "4029" ID number in upper left-hand corner of body at brakeman's platform.
(A) 1971-?, smooth MA1 roof; has simulated door to brakeman's platform.
    250
(B) 1972-74, MA2 roof (six seams); lacks door to brakeman's platform. Has also been seen with Low-Arched LA1 roof (no seams); possibly a post-factory substitution.
    225

An early variant on the original 4030 boxcar, 4029 was issued as a separately catalogued item, with a Medium-Arched roof initially smooth and then (1972) seamed, in contrast to the Low-Arched roof of 4030. The car was short-lived, discontinued in 1974.

4030: 1969-86, four-wheel boxcar (Gw class) of the Deutsche Reichsbahn. Sliding doors and brakeman's platform railings; body similar to 4029, but lacks simulated door to brakeman's platform; Low-Arched LA1 roof (six seams, two vents); filigree roof supports; "4030" embossed in upper left-hand corner of body end at brakeman's platform; length 300 mm.
(A) 1969-76, unpainted straw brown body; no body or frame markings. **155**

4030 has as long a production record as any car in the Lehmann line. It was unpainted and unlettered through 1976, but since then markings have slowly increased.

(B) 1977-80, unpainted light brown body; white detail markings on middle of first body panel next to brakeman's platform on slats six through nine; large "DR" heat-stamped above "4030" above "Gw" on sliding doors; Type 1 frame markings or frame markings absent. **68**
(C) 1981-82, same as (B), but with one white, square computer mark at each corner of body. **55**
(D) 1982-83, same as (C), but with "4030" painted on third slat of first panel next to brakeman's platform with marking added to bottom slat and markings at center of first panel reduced in size and limited to slats six, seven and eight; markings also added to bottom slat of last panel opposite brakeman's platform; Type 1 frame markings. **55**
(E) 1983-86, same as (D), but with "Deutsche Reichsbahn" on sliding doors in place of "DR"; Type 2 frame markings. **CP**

4030SB: 1984, Schmidt Bakery boxcar with four wheels; rich, chocolate brown boxcar same as 4030, but with white "Schmidt Lebkuchen aus Nurnberg" on each sliding door; white "4030" in upper side corner of body adjacent to brakeman's platform; sold with 20526 train set. **NSS**

4031: 1969-74, "Magnesium" boxcar with four wheels; unpainted body same as 4030, but in white color; Low-Arched LA1 roof (six seams, two roof vents); filigree roof supports; no frame markings. Some pieces may lack door decal (this should not dramatically change value). This car stayed in production long enough to receive E2 wheels and shaded roof; B. Cage comment.
(A) "MAGNESIUM" decal in black letters on sliding doors. **275**
(B) "MAGNESIT" decal on doors. **275**

4031: 1980-85, white soft drink reefer car with four wheels. Same body as 4030, but with "PEPSI" logo covering panels on end opposite brakeman's platform; large blue snowflake above the Lehmann logo and "Getranke-dienst"; miscellaneous black detail markings on first, second, third and sixth panels from brakeman's platform; two black computer markings at

For those who like sterner drink, 4031 comes with three peel-and-stick beer company labels, including a variant on the "Tucher" label of 4032, discontinued in 1980. Only a prototype was ever produced in the Coca-Cola version.

each corner; Low-Arched LA1 roof (six seams, two vents); filigree roof supports; comes with three different brewery signs (Kulmbacher EKU, Weihenstephan and Tucher) for conversion purposes; Type 1 or 2 frame markings. Some early cars came in 4031C Cola Cola boxes; B. Cage and J. Henderson comments. Length 300 mm. Note: Tucher label differs from 4032 in having smaller discs, facing toward the right rather than the left, with no "P.G.", blue background rather than white.   **CP**

4031C: 1984, uncatalogued "Cluss Brauerie Cluss Heilbronn" beer reefer car; white body with same detail and dimension markings as 4031 Pepsi car, but has Cluss billboard logo with company coat of arms above "Cluss" (in green and yellow) above "Brauerie Cluss Heilbronn" (in black) all surrounded by green and orange border; production limited to 100.   **NRS**

4031HS: 1984, four-wheel red-painted boxcar, same body as 4031 (4031 ID number), but with white "Freizeit Hobby Spiel" between door and brakeman's platform; two red, orange and white stripes, one of which passes horizontally from the brakeman's platform and angles diagonally across door while the other angles up body panels opposite brakeman's platform; company logo in red and orange on white between door and end opposite brakeman's platform; Low-Arched charcoal gray LA1 roof with black shading (six seams, two vents). Sold with 20513 train set.   **NSS**

After a hiatus from 1981 through 1984, the number of the old "Tucher" beer car was reassigned to this "Nestle's" chocolate car 4032. Both white; both fattening products; but different railings.

4032: 1973-80, Tucher Beer four-wheel reefer car (Tucher-Brauerei) with unpainted white-colored body, sliding doors and brakeman's platform; Low-Arched LA1 roof (six seams, two vents), filigree roof supports; length 300 mm. Not to be confused with 4031 with "Tucher" label applied; see note above, 4031, distinguishing labels.
(A) 1973-78, no markings on body except for large "Tucher Pils" sign covering body panels furthest from brakeman's platform; no frame markings.   **125**
(B) 1979-80, same as (A), but with black detail markings on body panel closest to brakeman's platform.   **85**
(C) 1979-80, same as (B), but with metal grab-irons between roof and brakeman's platform; Type 1 frame markings.   **100**

4032: 1985-86, Nestle Chocolate four-wheel boxcar painted white with a smooth, simulated metal sliding door on each side; markings on door include: black "Chocolate" above red "NESTLE" above black "PETER" above turquoise "Caillers" above blue "Kohler". The edges of the upper (two per side) and lower (one per side) vent grills are painted black. There are two black computer markers on the lower edges of each corner of the body; red dimension markings on first body panel next to brakeman's platform as well as "LGB" over "4032" over "K3" on second body panel next to brakeman's platform; MA3 roof.   **CP**

4032C: 1979-80, Coca Cola soft drink four-wheel reefer car; two versions of this car exist — one produced for LGB, the other for Primus. Possibly made up by Al Lentz who visited factory and brought back enough plaques to make up 10 cars. Plaques were for one side only, did not fit between vertical panels on other side; J. Hylva comment. Low-Arched LA1 roof (six seams, two vents).
(A) 1980, very similar to 4031 Pepsi car but has silk-screened "Coca Cola" logos on sides at end opposite brakeman's platform; no frame markings; made by Lehmann. This is probably one of the scarcest cars LGB has produced; B. Cage comment. Due to a reputed licensing problem, this car was advertised but very few produced before being withdrawn. Probably less than 25 reached U.S.   **450**

The earliest version of this recent car, made in 1984, was embossed 4031, but since then it has had its own number, 4034. The large roof vents presumably represent fans; Cardinal, of course, is a beer.

(B) 1979, similar to (A), but with Type 1 frame markings and black dimensional markings on one side only; no snowflake on door; made for Primus.   **400**
4032F: 1983, four-wheel boxcar, similar to 4032 soft drink car, with no markings on body, Low-Arched LA1 roof; sold originally with 20501F train set. Sold separately in Tucher beer boxes; B. Cage comment; or in 4032F stamped boxes in red; M. Richter Collection. May not have been issued by Lehmann; B. Roth comment.   **NRS**
(A) Florsheim decal in gold and white on end opposite brakeman's platform.   **65**
(B) Florsheim decal placed over red plaque with decal end door; may be prototype. J. Hylva Collection.   **NRS**
4032L: 1980-84, Lowenbrau beer four-wheel reefer car; refrigerated wagon with brakeman's platform and two large vent fans on roof; white body with light blue "LOWENBRAU" over "MUNCHEN" on second and third panels from brakeman's platform and on sliding door; Lowenbrau lion logo covering panels furthest from brakeman's platform; other brewery decals available; Low-Arched LA1 roof (six seams, two vents), filigree roof support; length 300 mm; Type 1 or 2 frame markings; discontinued in 1984.
(A) 1980-81, embossed "4031" identification number in upper left-hand corner of end body panel at brakeman's platform; unpainted body; usually came in a yellow box with window display; Type 1 or 2 frame markings.   **85**
(B) 1981-84, "4032" identification number; unpainted body; no markings or decals; sold only in red boxes; Type 2 or 3 frame markings.   **80**
(C) 1984, same as (B), but with painted body. May also have been issued as a version of (A); reader comments requested.   **80**
4033: 1973-85, yellow "Chiquita" banana boxcar with sliding doors and brakeman's platform; yellow color may vary, some earlier pieces being light, faded yellow rather than the typical bright slightly orangish-yellow; positions of markings on car body may vary slightly from descriptions; Low-Arched LA1 roof (six seams two vents), vents large (fans) or small; filigree roof supports; length 300 mm. Sold separately and with 20401 train set until 1984; thereafter sold only with set.
(A) 1973, body markings limited to peel-and-stick door emblems with the "Chiquita" name in white; no frame markings.   **NRS**
(B) 1973, same as (A), but without "Chiquita" emblem.   **NRS**
(C) 1974-76, heat-stamped white dimension markings on body panel closest to brakeman's platform; same peel-and-stick "Chiquita" door emblems as (A); metal grab-irons link platform railings to roof on some pieces; Type 1 frame markings on some pieces. Questionable existence; J. Barton comment.   **100**

The yellow 4033 Chiquita Banana car, whose "Chiquita" has come, and gone, and changed, now is available only with set 20401.

The special issue Vedes car, 4033V, seems out of place with the much older cars around it; its slogan translates more or less "We travel for play and holiday." Below it is the 4029, with its Medium-Arched roof, and the 4030, with its Low-Arched roof. At right, note the patriotic colors of two 4040As and a 4040E, all with the older long tank bodies. The handles at the end of the purge valve extension pipes show at left of the bottom two tankers as white and red circles, respectively, overlapping the profiles of the larger purge valves. A Rudman Collection.

(D) 1974-76, same as (C), but without "Chiquita" emblem. **90**

(E) 1977-79, same peel-and-stick "Chiquita" door emblems as (A); black heat-stamped dimension markings; "4033" and other markings added to the first panel next to brakeman's platform; one black computer marking at each corner of body; no metal grab-irons between roof and railings of brakeman's platform; Type 1 frame markings. **60**

(F) 1977-79, same as (E), but without "Chiquita" emblem. **58**

(G) 1982-86, similar to (E), but with silk-screened door emblem with the "Chiquita" name in yellow; Chiquita emblem slightly rounder at top and bottom; black-painted vent grate at base of first panel next to brakeman's platform (this was not painted on earlier versions) and two square-shaped computer markings at each corner of body; Type 1 or 2 frame markings. **CP**

4033B: 1983, uncatalogued; Brinkman boxcar; yellow body with same dimension and weight markings as 4033(G), but has blue and white billboard signs with the octagonal Brinkman Company logo and name attached to each side of body at end opposite brakeman's platform; sold only with set 20516 **NSS**

4033V: 1984, uncatalogued; Vedes Company four-wheel boxcar; orange-yellow-painted body; green "Wir fahren Fur Spiel Freizeit" across the sliding door and a stationary door logo with "Vedes Fachgeschafte" black "4031P" in upper side corner of body adjacent to brakeman's platform; other numbers and identification in black; Low-Arched LA1 roof (six seams, two vents); Type 3 frame markings; only about 500 (1,000; B. Roth comment) made. **100**

4034: 1984-86, a 4031 series reefer having an unpainted yellow body with "Cardinal" in large black letters across three panels next to brakeman's platform with black "2897p/HK-v/9,ot/6450kg"; large logo plaque on body panels opposite brakeman's platform has two red-painted figures outlined in black toasting one another over a beer barrel; Low-Arched LA1 roof (six seams, two vents), with filigree supports; solid ends, two sliding doors on sides.

(A) 1984, embossed "4031" identification number in upper left-hand corner of end body panel at brakeman's platform. Sold only with set 20512. **NSS**

(B) 1985-86, same as (A), but with "4034" identification number. **CP**

Owner Wolfgang Richter has said that circus car 4036 is only the first in an intended series of circus cars. But for the moment, circus train fanciers must be content to expand their trains with such post-production modifications as those of the Rheinberger Company. A lion, elephant, ape, camel, rhinoceros, polar bear and a trainer are playful accessories for the circus car, assortment 5027 (seven pieces.)

4035: 1980-86, boxcar originally of the Wurttemberg narrow-gauge line for express freight of the Mosbach-Mudau Railway, which became part of the DB in more recent years. Sliding doors; regulation markings which include one square white computer mark at each corner of body; black chalkboard on each side; no brakeman's platform; Low-Arched LA2 roof (no seams, no vents; textured); length 300 mm. **CP**

4036: 1985-86, circus boxcar with grillwork on sliding side doors; body is similar to the 4035 four-wheel boxcar. The circus car is painted white with the word "CIRCUS" painted in blue, yellow and red on each side to the right of the side door; black "Altenfurt/Fischbahn", blue "4036" and the black "message board" are on each side of the body to the left of door. Each body side has eleven five-pointed stars (five to the left of door and six to the right) in blue, red and yellow. Although the chassis depicted in the 1984-85 catalogue is painted blue without painted marking, production versions have Type C frame markings; Low-Arched LA2 roof (no seams, no vents; textured). Includes animal loading ramp. **CP**

4063: 1973-86, eight-wheel boxcar (GGm/s type) with twin-axle trucks of the Pinzgau Local Railway. Brakeman's cab doors and four sliding doors actually open; Low-Arched LA3 roof (ten seams, rails for sliding doors); FA3

railing (Frame of Angle iron, half freestanding, half cast on brakeman's hut); length 430 mm.

(A) 1973, earliest version is straw brown-colored without markings on body or frame; FA3(A) railing (relief brake pipe and hose). **100**

(B) 1973-74, same as (A), but with four small body markings on the 11th through 14th slats of the panel closest to the brakeman's platform. **100**

(C) 1975-78, same as (B), but in darker brown color. **90**

(D) 1979-82, darker brown color with "OBB" over "GGSm" over "16818", all on the lower half of the second body panel from the brakeman's platform; during this period FA3(A) railings (relief brake pipe and hose changed to FA3(B) railings (freestanding brake pipe and hose). **75**

(E) 1983-86, similar to (D), but with markings on second panel from brakeman's platform slightly higher on panel and the addition of "4063LGB" above vent grate at center side of body; nine frame markings are added at eight intervals along the frame. **CP**

4064: 1977-80, eight-wheel wooden-sided refrigerator car of the Denver & Rio Grande Western Railroad. Twin-axle, arch bar trucks; body has separately cast grab-irons and ice hatch latches; opening, double-leaf side doors; LA4 roof (peaks at center, 12 seams, catwalk); length 415 mm.

A companion to gondola 4062, boxcar 4063, like most Lehmann standard brown cars, has darkened somewhat in the several versions since its 1973 introduction. The separated pair of doors is an unusual feature of the prototype Pinzgau Railway cars.

75

An assortment of American cars: 4067 is shown in two liveries, top left (C) and bottom right (D); the current version (E) is a darker brown and lettered D&RGW. 4064, top right, has its separately attached grab-irons contrasting to the relief grab-irons of the cars around it; the presence (rare) or absence (common) of white markings on the ends determines whether the car is 4064(B) or 4064(C). A very close look at the letter on its open slats distinguishes this 4068(E), lower left, from the (C) of almost a decade earlier, for the newer cattle cars' interior height ("I.H.") is "6 FT.1 3/4 IN." rather than "6 FT.1 1/4 IN.".

(A) 1977-78, bright yellow body sides; medium brown painted ends and roof; ice hatches and catwalks around them are beige-colored; black markings on sides include "D&RGW" above "56" on left-hand portions and "REFRIGERATOR" above and slightly to the left of the detail markings in the lower right-hand corner region; the brown ends each have a small, white "D&RGW" over "56" in the upper right-hand corner. This version is shown in the 1977-78 catalogue but confirmation is requested. **400**

(B) 1979-80, body is entirely bright yellow; gray roof, some may have black shaded edges; white markings which include "D&RGW" over "4064" on left portion while the right-hand portion has a Denver & Rio Grande Western logo above and to the right of the word "REFRIGERATOR" which, in turn, is situated above and to the left of the detail markings in the lower right-hand corner; the ends of the body have specification markings at lower center and "D&RGW" above "4064" in the upper right-hand corner. This version is shown in the 1979-80 catalogue but confirmation is requested.

Brakewheel partially blocks lettering on one side of car; G. Nicholson comment. J. Barton, B. Cage and J. Hylva Collections. **200**

(C) 1979-80, uncatalogued; very similar to (B), but without white markings on ends of body. This is the most common version of this car. $115-$120 West coast price, $150-$155 East coast price; B. Henderson comment. **165**

4067: 1974-86, eight-wheel wooden-sided boxcar with twin-axle arch bar trucks; sliding door on each side and catwalk and brakeman's wheel on roof; embossed grab-irons; LA4 roof (peaks at center, 12 seams, catwalk); length 415 mm. This car may have been produced in two body variations: the 1974-75 catalogue shows the vent cover plates on the body sides with latches; the sliding vent doors on the ends have a horizontal strap across the middle. The large sliding doors are also shown to have an additional handle on the left-hand edge. The vent cover plates on the sides of the later versions (1977 and newer) are smaller and have simulated latches and the sliding vent doors on the ends lack the horizontal strap.

The D&RG boxcar 4067 may have some unconfirmed body variation, but definitely was issued in three colors: yellow, medium brown and a darker brown.

The open slats identify 4068's prototype as a stock car. Since 1974, it has appeared in three shades of green, and various letterings. Europeans, shipping their cattle shorter distances (such as to high meadows during summer), often use cars such as 4030, with its small closable vents on each side, rather than the porous slats of this American car.

(A) 1974-77?, bright yellow-colored body same as 4064; gray roof and catwalk; brakewheel shaft is black all the way down the end of the body; black markings include "D&RGW" above "4067" on the left-hand portion of the body sides. This version is listed in the 1974-75 catalogue and may also have been produced with white markings. Confirmation is requested for both versions. **NRS**
(B) 1974?, unpainted gray body without markings; unusual prototype version. J. Hylva Collection. **NRS**
(C) 1977-78, same color as (A), but with black catwalk and black shading on roof; white "4067" above "CAPY 40000" above "LT. WT. 17900 KLR 4 34" on the side of the body to the left of the door; "SOUTHERN PACIFIC LINES" circular logo to the right of the door on the upper portion. **150**
(D) 1978, similar to (C) but roof is painted medium brown. R. Enners Collection. **NRS**
(E) 1979, unpainted medium brown body, no markings. J. Hylva Collection. **250**
(F) 1979-84, unpainted medium brown body; same markings as (C), but with additional markings (which may vary) "NHM (9)" over "17 11 26.83"

in the lower side corner to the right of the door. Some later 1984 versions have a lighter gray roof; G. Nicholson comment. **75**
(G) 1984-85, D&RG version, similar to (F), but with darker brown body; white "D&RG" to the left of the sliding door and "4067" on the door itself. **70**
(H) 1985-86, D&RG version, same color as (E) with markings similar to (G) but has additional plaque molded on body just left center of doors; plaque reads, "FLOUR SUGAR AND BEAN LOADING ONLY"; other markings added include "NEW ROOF" above "ALA-6-24" and door has "L" and "DO NOT CLEAT DOOR" at bottom. Roof is painted greenish-gray with black edging. **CP**
4068: 1974-86, narrow gauge, eight-wheel stock car of the Denver & Rio Grande Western Railroad. Green-colored body with ventilated sides and sliding doors; catwalk and brakewheel are on a LA4 roof (peaks at center, 12 seams); length 415 mm.
(A) 1974, green body; bright gray unpainted roof and catwalk; the horizontal slat with white "D&RGW" is situated at the horizontal center of the box body (this is lower on more recent versions); the only other marking

The Budweiser car, 4070, features a billboard side popular in the United States in the early part of this century, before the ICC's outlawing of such advertising (rescinded not long ago). The car has been in production four years; variations are slight. Unlike 4067, 4070 has freestanding grab-irons.

When Lehmann's plans for a 4031 Coca-Cola car fell through, apparently for inability to reach a satisfactory arrangement on the use of the copyrighted name, American importer Lawton Jordon (Cimmaron Ltd.) was able to negotiate an eight-wheel American prototype Coca-Cola billboard reefer, 4072.

is "4068" beneath "D&RGW"; black brakewheel shaft is a separate piece attached to the end of the body. It is likely that this version was a prototype and not put into production in this exact form. However, a version may have been produced with similar markings using the commonly known body-type with embossed brakewheel shaft and slat for "D&RGW" just below horizontal center of body (see (C)). Prototype model.   **NRS**

(B) 1974-?, unpainted gray body; no markings; unusual prototype version. J. Hylva Collection.   **NRS**

(C) 1974-75, uncatalogued; unpainted medium green body; brakeshaft details are embossed below roof line; all markings are heat-stamped and include horizontal slat with white "D&RGW" situated just below the horizontal center of box body; "4068" has a small "D" next to the upper portion of the "8"; white "Rio Grande" is on horizontal slat just above horizontal center of right-hand portion of box body; "ALA. 12 49" (below "4068"), "CAPY 50000", "LD.LMT.55000" and "LT. WT. 22700" on left-hand portion of body; "REBUILT 26", "CU. FT. 1312", "I.L. 29 FT.4 IN.", "I.W.7 FT.3 IN." and "I.H.6 FT.1-1/4 IN." on right-hand portion of body; black catwalk; gray roof with black shading at edges. R. Enners Collection.   **NRS**

(D) 1975-76, similar markings to (C) but painted on; body is unpainted dark green (color similar to current version).   **135**

(E) 1979, medium green-painted body, no markings. J. Hylva Collection.   **275**

(F) 1977-82, same markings as (D), but with medium green-painted body, lighter than (A) or (D).   **80**

(G) 1983-86, uncatalogued; same markings as (D), except reads "I.H. 6 FT. 1 3/4 IN.", but with dark green-painted body; deceptively similar to (D).   **CP**

4070: 1982-85, Budweiser beer reefer car with same basic body as 4064; unpainted white plastic car body; brown-painted roof and ends; black "Anheuser-Busch" over red and white "BUDWEISER" logo above black "King of all bottled beers." to the left of doors; black "STLR & CO" over "4070" on doors; yellow "Anheuser-Busch" over eagle logo above black "BEER CAR" to the right of doors; LA4 roof (peaks at center, 12 seams, catwalk); length 415 mm.

(A) 1982-84, yellow "Anheuser-Busch" and light-colored details on logo all to the right of doors; "A" in logo is red without black shadowing.   **CP**

(B) 1982-85, goldenrod "Anheuser-Busch" and light-colored details on logo all to the right of doors; "A" in logo is red with black shadowing.   **CP**

4070BTO: 1981, same basic body as 4070, but unpainted white as a special issue for the 1981 LGB Model RR Club annual car; has decals to celebrate the LGB Model RR Club convention at Strasburg, Pennsylvania; only 100 made.

(A) With decals, 50 made.   **145**

(B) Without decals, 50 made; B. Cage comment.   **100**

4070NC: 1984-85, Tiffany eight-wheel reefer car; custom painted white with light gold markings for North Coast Distributors of Medina, Ohio; not produced by Lehmann.   **90**

4071: 1984, REA (Railway Express Agency) limited issue reefer; same basic body style as 4064; dark green-painted body; brown-painted LA4 roof (peaks at center, 12 seams, catwalk), with black edging; gold "REFRIGER-ATOR" above a red and white diamond-shaped "RAILWAY EXPRESS AGENCY" sign on left-hand portion of body; gold "RAILWAY EXPRESS AGENCY" and "REX 4071" on right-hand portion of body; gray side frames on arch bar trucks. Only about 2000 made. Lettering may be of American manufacture or application; confirmation requested.   **125**

4072: 1985, uncatalogued; eight-wheel Coca Cola reefer car manufactured by Lehmann for Cimmaron, Ltd. of Atlanta, Georgia; same basic body and roof as 4064, but with glossy red-painted body; "Enjoy Coca-Cola" logo to the left of sliding doors and "COKE IS IT" to the right of doors; black door hinges on opening door, five black step rungs on right, one on lower middle left; came in gray sleeve with white "COKE / Model Train / Limited Edition" on Coke red background label; silver-painted roof; gray side frames on arch bar trucks. Only 2000 made.   **135**

4074: 1985-86, Pabst beer reefer with eight wheels; similar to 4064 reefer; body is painted yellow with brown ends; roof painted brown; body markings include green "PABST" above black "MILWAUKEE" above black "U.R.T. CO.91021" to the left of side doors; to the right of the side doors is a round-shaped logo with the words "PABST MILWAUKEE" on a red ring with a black outside edge, all of which surrounds a white center with a green leaf with a large, white letter "B" on it; black "Pabst-ette" above "MALT SYRUP BEVERAGES" are to the right of the logo; below these markings are the following dimension markings in black: "CAPY 60000" above "LD. LMT. 788000" above "LT. WT. 57200" above "ICE CAPY. 8550".   **CP**

Like 4070, 4074 is based on the out-of-production 4064. Its ice hatches and center opening doors are typical of vintage American reefers.

Chapter IX
Tank Cars

Early and late tank car ends, the older ones in the center. The new and old at left are the valveless ends of a 4040E and a 4040S. Notice how much wider the old cars are, mounted as they are on standard flatcars, with their ladders angled out rather than vertical and, of course, their operating side valves reaching far out to clear the decks. At center right is the purge valve end of an old blue 4040A, with its long extension to the side; and at the far right is the equivalent end of a new 4040RZ, with its short tank. C. Colwell Collection.

The LGB tank cars were produced in two basic versions all of which have four wheels (two axles) and measure 300 mm in total length. Those pieces produced from 1969 to 1978 have longer tanks, the caps at each end of the main tank body extend about 45 millimeters from the seam to the terminal bulge, and the purge drain at the end (not the side-mounted spout) has an additional pipe and valve jutting off to one side. These earlier tank versions are mounted on a bed similar to the 4000 black flatcar. This early variation is designated as the ET-type (for "early tank") in the descriptions below. The decals with company emblems and names for tanks were generally not put on at the factory but were packed with each car to be put on by the purchaser. Therefore placement of decals may vary or they may be absent. The more recently produced tank cars have

shorter tanks, the cap at each end of the main body extends only about 25 millimeters from the seam to the terminal bulge, the purge drain lacks the additional pipe and valve, hold-down lugs secure the dome tread plates. The tank is mounted on platform sections, one with brake handle and FA2 railing (Frame of Angle iron, two inverted "U"s with low crossmembers joined by a permanently raised tread plate; freestanding brake hose and pipe), specifically designed for this car which, in turn, is mounted on a typical 300 mm chassis. From 1979-1982, a single pair of lugs holds one end of the tread assembly to the tank top; since 1983, a second pair secures the other end as well. This more recent version, first catalogued in 1979, is designated as the LT-type (for "late tank") in the descriptions. Company emblems are painted, in place of the earlier decals. Pieces to look for are possible transition cars that may have had the ET body with the more recent markings.

The end cap of this ET 4040A protrudes far enough to eliminate an end platform, not possible until the tanks were shortened. The car came in three colors, gray, white and blue.

4040: 1969-70, oil car with "Petroleum" decal on each side of tank generally to the left of the fill dome; no other tank markings; ET-type, gray-colored tank; no frame markings.
(A) 1969-70, gray-colored tank.   **450**
(B) 1970, white-colored tank.   **350**
(C) 1970, white-colored tank, "Dortmunder Hansa Bier" decals; this is a "one-of-a-kind" car that was produced as an experimental prototype. J. Hylva Collection.   **NRS**
4040: 1984, unpainted white LT tank car; no markings on tank. 500 sold to United States distributors for custom repainting, but many were retailed "as is" in blank form. Some were advertised for sale as 4040W.   **78**
4040A: 1969-78, Aral tank car; several versions are known to have been produced from 1969 to 1978 only in the ET tank-type.

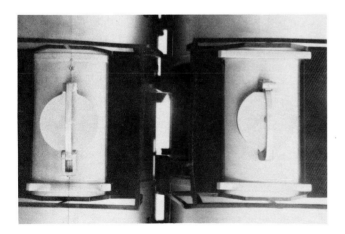

When the shorter late tanks were introduced to the 4040 series tank cars in 1979, a horizontal bar, tapered at the ends, was cast onto one of the bands encircling the tank at the catwalk by the filler dome: the bar's two projecting ends hooked the catwalk tread, helping to hold it and its attached ladders in place. By 1983, a second bar with its pair of lugs was being added to the band on the other side of the dome. C. Colwell Collection.

Tank cars changed most obviously in tank length, which was shortened in 1978-1979. Above, the older style: 4040BP with 4040A (which also came in white and gray versions), and 4040S with 4040E. Other changes included a special open frame, replacing the flatcar body, with end railing on the platform permitted by the shorter tank: 4040S(E), the black Shell tank car made for Primus; two of the half dozen or so 4040Cs — the all silver 4040C(A), and the wide-banded 4040C(E); and "4040W", a limited American import intended for refinishing but often marketed unpainted and unlettered.

The new 4040BP, black rather than green. The end drain valve extension is missing from the LT's; a dummy valve is centered on the off side. Marker boards on the side, for which peel-and-stick colored labels are provided, are another difference between the older and newer tank cars.

(A) 1969-70, gray-colored tank, same as 4040, but with blue and white diamond-shaped Aral emblem; no other tank markings; no frame markings. May have "petroleum" decal on each side; Colwell comment. **425**

(B) 1971-76, same as (A), but with white-colored tank; black base, black spigot on tank, black ladder and walkway around cap on top. **285**

(C) 1977-78, same as (A), but with light blue-colored tank. **185**

(D) 1979, a four-axle version in medium blue; brakeman's platform, with fill dome off-center toward that end; a composite of two LT tanks. Has been identified as a prototype; closely resembles Rheinberger post-factory modification car #R-4480. R. Enners Collection. **NRS**

4040B: 1971-74 and 1982-86, BP (British Petroleum) Mineral Oil Company tank car; produced in at least three versions from 1971 to 1974, re-introduced in 1982.

(A) 1971-74, green-colored tank, ET-type; BP logo is in the form of a green shield with yellow "BP" letters on a large white square that is situated on sides of tank generally to the left of the fill dome; C. Colwell comment. **375**

(B) 1973-74, same as (A), but tank is olive-green. **350**

(C) Circa 1981, Al Lentz offered a limited number of LT tank cars painted a deep, glossy bluish-green with "BP" stickers, yellow letters on a green shield on a white background, through the BTO Newsletter of the LGB Club; not a Lehmann finish. **NRS**

(D) 1982-83, flat black-painted tank, LT-type; green BP shield with yellow "BP" on a large white square with rounded corners is situated to the right of the fill dome. Note: Copies are now on the market with phony white field decals on the side; G. Nicholson comment. **115**

(E) 1983-86, uncatalogued; same as (B), but without white, square field around BP shield. **CP**

4040C(B), distinguished by its very narrow black band. The new, narrow open frame for the LT types narrows the extremely wide loading gauge required by the working spigot on the old ET types, which had to reach far out to clear the wide decking of the flatcar base.

The end of the newer 4040E (and other LT tankers) is short enough for a platform and its special angle iron railing. All 4040s may be filled through the hinged cap on top and drained through the working spigot at the side.

4040C: 1978-86, BASF chemical tank car as used by the RhB; produced only in the LT tank-type in at least six versions; black ladder and walkway, black base, black valve handle.

(A) 1978-79, silver-painted tank over gray plastic; small white-lettered "BASF" peel-and-stick decal, black rectangle with silver letters, generally situated to right of fill dome, gray plastic spout; no other tank markings; detail markings present on display boards; Type 1 frame markings. **80**

(B) 1979-80, same as (A), but with 20 mm wide black band at vertical center of tank reaching from just below fill dome to lowest horizontal seam. **75**

(C) 1981-82, uncatalogued; similar to (A) and (B), but with slightly wider black band about 30 mm that reaches from about 20 mm below fill dome and to about 5 mm above lowest horizontal seam; small white and black rectangular warning sign in upper portion of black band; white-lettered "BASF" emblem is slightly larger than in (A) or (B). Type 1 frame markings. **58**

(D) Same as (C), but black rectangle is painted on with BASF letters in silver; computer markings on ends of tanks. **55**

(E) 1983-84, silver color on tank enhanced by clear, glossy finish; black band is very wide, covers area between the two vertical seams just beneath catwalks around fill dome; silver-lettered "BASF" emblem similar to (D); two black computer marks at each corner of tank, one rectangle over one pentagle. **CP**

(F) 1985-86, same as (D), but without glossy finish. **CP**

4040E: 1971-86, Esso Oil Company tank car; produced in at least three versions.

(A) 1971-78, ET tank-type in unpainted semi-gloss red color with blue, white and red oval-shaped "ESSO" emblem situated to the left of the fill dome; no additional tank markings or frame markings; black stairs and walkway around hatch, black fill spigot handle. **175**

(B) 1979-83, white LT-type body with the same "ESSO" oval emblem in the same position as in (A), but tank has a 25 x 100 mm red stripe at the horizontal center on the center and right sections of tank; Type 1 or 2 frame markings. **48**

(C) 1983-86, uncatalogued; same as (B), but with two square computer marks at each corner of tank. **CP**

4040S: 1971-86, Shell Oil Company tank car; this yellow-colored tanker appears to have been produced in at least three variations.

(A) 1971-78, semi-glossy yellow ET-type tank with company emblem comprised of the "SHELL" name in red letters across a yellow sea shell, surrounded by a square-shaped red field; this emblem is situated to the left

of the fill dome; black stairs, walkaround and valve handle, black simulated wooden base; steps at four corners on end sides. **165**

(B) 1979-82, same yellow color as (A) in LT-type tank; company emblem comprised of a yellow sea shell bordered in red which follows contour of shell and the "SHELL" name is in large red letters along horizontal middle in the center and right-hand tank sections; Type 1 or 2 frame markings; no square-shaped computer marks at each corner of tank. **85**

(C) 1983-86, uncatalogued; same as (B), but with two square-shaped computer marks at each corner of tank. **CP**

(D) 1979-80, black unpainted tank car, same decal as in (A), but LT-type made for Primus. **100**

(E) ET model was produced for Primus as shell car with matte black tank, red and yellow shell sticker; B. Cage comment. **100**

4040RZ: 1984, uncatalogued, red-painted LT body-type; green and yellow "LGB" logo on white stripe to the left of fill dome; sold only with the 20401RZ train set; however some were broken up and sold separately. **55**

Note: A white tank car lettered "Sudfunk" has been reported; no further information available. Reader comment requested.

4040BTO: 1979, very similar to 4040C(D), but "BASF" label replaced with special decals for the LGB Model RR Club "BTO" convention car for 1979; only 75 were made. **135**

A tank car in transition, the gray 4040 petroleum car is on its way to becoming a white 4040A Aral car. The typically long tank of this early ET tank car came with "Petroleum" decals attached, and with "Aral" peel-and-stick emblems loose in the box. C. Colwell Collection

Chapter X

Powered Railcars, Short Cars (170 mm),
Service Wagons and Cable Cars

Left: As the pump handles rise and fall, the workman's arms swing and he rocks back and forth. 2001 has no couplers or pickup slider; color of the deck has varied.

Right: The 3041 excursion car's roof darkened in 1979 and even more in 1981; the red body darkened in 1984. The car has been featured in set 300 with a battery locomotive, and in starter set 20701T.

Left: The 3530 tower wagon with rotating platform, for servicing overhead wires, has gone through several changes in its browns and blacks and warning markings. One of the more conspicuous changes was the addition of the plaque on the side of the ladder, in 1982.

Right: Tipping bucket 4043 has remained virtually unchanged since a slight color variation in 1974. Like other short cars, it has appeared in low cost starter sets.

Early catalogues list these very short cars as 150 mm long, but they are now more accurately identified as 170 mm. Typically, they are special purpose cars (cable, wine, excursion) and are found on very short prototype lines.

2001: 1971-86, powered track inspection handcar, brown sides, yellow or tan bed, green toolbox; red wheels; man pumps handle as car moves; no electrical pickup skates; length 140 mm.
(A) 1971-72, large toolbox, small wheels (visible through sides with running boards), no oil drums. Very rare; J. Barton comment.   **NRS**
(B) 1973-86, small toolbox, large wheels, two oil drums, tools on bed. Earlier versions had fewer painted parts and the lever and its supports were in dull red. Otherwise these cars have been unchanged.   **CP**
3041: 1974-86, four-wheel summer-type, open passenger coach with grab-handles as used on tramway, park, exhibition and beach railways. A flattened TA3 roof (tapered toward edges and ends, two roof vents); length 150 mm.
(A) 1974-78, no "3041" number painted on ends; embossed designs in ends unpainted; curtains painted white; very light whitish-gray roof.   **35**
(B) 1979-80, similar to (A), but curtains more fully painted with black cross-hatchings; medium gray roof.   **30**
(C) 1981-83, similar to (B), but with white and black "3041" on ends; embossed designs on ends painted white.   **25**
(D) 1984-86, similar to (C), but main body painted deep red.   **CP**
3510: 1977-82, a short, open gondola for maintenance work; has red and white safety markings and brake crank; length 150 mm.
(A) 1977-78, bright yellow gondola body with red and white peel-and-stick safety markings pointing downward at corners. May be prototype.   **NRS**
(B) 1978-79, lighter yellow gondola body than (A) with red and white-painted safety markings pointing upward at corners.   **34**
(C) 1979-82, same color body as (A), but with same safety markings as (B).   **28**
3530: 1977-86, tower wagon for servicing catenary systems; with pivot table work platform, tool chest and ladders; length 170 mm.
(A) 1977-78, red and white safety markings cover lower edge of sides on pivot table work platform; no additional markings; light brown tower portion including work platform ladders and tool chest; tan bed and black chassis.   **38**
(B) 1979-80, similar to (A), but with yellow and black safety markings limited only to lower corners of pivot table work platform; dark brown tower

portion including work platform and tool chest; black ladder; orange-brown flat bed; came in yellow box.   **35**
(C) 1981-86, similar to (A), but with red and white safety markings with small rectangular moving sign on each side all the way around lower edge of pivot table work platform; white-painted upper rail of work platform; large black rectangular sign with red, orange, yellow, white and black lettering is added to side of tower opposite the ladder.   **CP**
4042: 1971-86, four-wheel "Matra-Frankfurt" service crane car; crane cars were used by railways to clear blocked track, for rail or bridge construction or for general loading. Yellow body and boom; operating boom and hook; crane base can be rotated 360 degrees; tool chest has opening, latching doors; length 300 mm.
(A) 1971-73, no marking other than red and white hazard stripes on end corners of toolbox; boom has early "snap-catch" for jib extension on end of boom.   **NRS**
(B) 1974-78, red and white hazard stripes on all four corners of toolbox; boom has white markings just above hydraulic ram; Matra label in black letters on white rectangle on each side of car just below base of crane; frame markings limited to "ges. Tragfahigkeit 20t".   **90**
(C) 1979-81, similar to (B), but with black markings on boom above hydraulic ram that include weight and angle charts; black and white arrows and triangles; doors of toolbox have black, red and white markings; Matra label in blue letters on white rectangle on each side of car just below base of crane.   **75**
(D) 1982-84, same as (C), but with "snap-catch" replaced by internal friction catch and a trigger support to secure boom in several upright positions.   **65**
(E) 1984-86, similar to (D), but with internal friction catch and a trigger support to secure boom in several positions; white markings on black portion of boom.   **CP**
4043: 1971-86, tipping bucket car that can be emptied by tipping the bucket to either side or bucket may be completely removed; length 170 mm.
(A) 1971-74, dull red plastic bucket.   **25**
(B) 1974-86, shiny red plastic bucket; slightly lighter than (A), but some of the earlier pieces were produced in reddish-pink.   **CP**
4044: 1974-86, short, high-sided gondola or ore car; simulated wood-grained gondola sides; with brake crank; generally sold with three oil drums; length 170 mm.
(A) 1974, unpainted straw brown gondola portions; white markings which include the "4044" on upper left end on each lateral side along with

The Rhaetian Railway operates a crane similar to 4042 (shown here), a fully hand-operable model with rotating extendable boom and crank-operated hook cable. The original in 1971 had no lettering; the type of extension boom lock has changed, and a boom support trigger has been added.

embossed "LGB" plate logo and "Sulzbach-Rosenburg"; black chassis and brake handle.   **35**

(B) 1974-75, similar to (A), but yellow; no ID number; sold with set 20601. D. Doggett Collection.   **NRS**

(C) 1976-84, same as (A), but with orange-brown gondola.   **26**

(D) 1983-84, yellow gondola as in 3510 service wagon; without safety markings on corners; red-brown simulated "LGB" plate logo "Sulzbach-Rosenburg"; "4044" number; available with the 20602 starter set. Some lack lead weight in chassis; R. Rench comment.   **30**

(E) 1984-86, orange-painted gondola with whitish-gray interior; yellow and red hazard stripes on corners pointing downward; black dimensional and detail markings.   **CP**

(F) Same as (D) but white and red corner markings.   **CP**

(G) Same as (E) and (F) but no corner markings and no grey interior. J. Barton Collection.   **CP**

(H) 1982-82, unpainted red gondola with no painted or embossed markings. This car is not a Lehmann product but a cheaper imitation made in Taiwan.
                                                                     4

4045: 1975-86, short stanchion wagon with bulkheads at each end and three stanchions, cast as part of body, on each side; originally sold with three to five blue or red oil drums; length 170 mm.

(A) Prior to 1974, uncatalogued, but visible in a photo scene of accessories for battery set 300 on page eight, 1979-80 catalogue, reprinted in the next three catalogues; gray stanchion body.   **65**

(B) 1973? 1975?, preproduction test run of 15 to 25: yellow stanchions and body. C. Colwell Collection.   **NRS**

(C) 1974, similar to 4042 shown above, but in dark green, unpainted plastic. H. Betruger Collection.   **NRS**

(D) 1975-76, straw brown stanchions and body.   **35**

(E) 1979-85, medium brown stanchions and body.   **CP**

4046: 1974-85, short cable wagon or cable jimmy with a single cable spool, rotatable on support stand; spool and/or stand can be removed from bed; discontinued in 1985; length 170 mm.

(A) 1974-75, very dark green spool on light tan support; dark brown bed; no markings.   **45**

(B) 1974-75, same as (A), but with black support.   **35**

(C) 1976-82, medium green spool; black support; orange-brown bed.   **28**

(D) 1982, same as (C), but with white and black markings on green spool.
                                                                     28

(E) 1985, yellow spool with same white and black markings as (D); medium brown bed.   **CP**

4047: 1974-86, wine wagon for providing water (or wine?) at construction sites; cask can be filled and tap utilized; length 170 mm.

(A) 1974-78, medium dark green cask top cap, drain plug and cask supports; yellow tap; black-painted barrel hoops around cask; dark brown bed; may be prototype.   **NRS**

(B) 1979-80, cask very dark green (nearly olive-green); black top cap, drain plug and cask supports on an orange-brown bed; unpainted hoops.   **50**

(C) 1980, light tan-colored cask; dark brown tap, fill plug and barrel hoops; black cask supports; rectangular white signs with black eagle and shield; red and black lettering on white placed with "Ferninand" over "Pieroth GM"

Top: Now orange, 4044 was in 1983-1984 briefly yellow, like the similar 3510, and before that was two shades of brown. Sold originally with blue Aral oil barrels, more recently also with red Esso barrels.

Left: Like 4044, 4045 is sold with oil drums. The gray version antedates 1975; although uncatalogued, it has appeared in the same catalogue picture, as background, from 1979 through 1985.

Right: Like its larger brothers, the 4040 gasoline tankers, 4047 can be filled from the top and emptied through a working spigot. Cask color and plaque are the major variants.

with "BH" under "GM", over "Weingut-Weinkellerei"; to the right of the shield, "Burg Layen" over "bei Bingen" over "am Rhein-Nahe Eck"; added to each side of cask; medium brown bed. May be a limited test run; reader comment requested.   **28**

(D) 1980-85, same as (C), but with dark orange-brown cask; eagle is filled in gold, shield in blue.   **CP**

(E) 1984, commemorative convention car favor, same as (C), but with silver cask; side boards proclaiming "1984-LGB Chicago" on side of cask; J. Hylva, J. Henderson and R. Rench comments. Production limited to about 40 pieces.   **NRS**

Cable cars typify the mountainous regions of Europe in which narrow gauge trains thrive. Set 9000S is the two cabin electrified version of Lehmann's cable cars, named for Mount Rigi, its top reachable from one side by narrow gauge cog railway, from the other by cable cars larger than but similar to these; the summit offers a 180 degree panorama of snowcapped Alps. Earlier sets were lithographed tinware, like many of Lehmann's older toys, rather than plastic.

4049: 1986, four-wheel searchlight and repair car "Hilfszuge-Wagon"; has small brown-painted workshop on one end with hand-operated search-light on the other; a rotating work platform on a tower similar to the 3530 repair car is situated in the middle of the bed. Light is robust and usable by children.   **CP**

4075: No production date set, searchlight and workshop wagon; a railway service car with open platforms, a gray-colored service compartment and guardrails; bridge with four searchlights and a scaffold; High-Arched roof with smokestack has flashing warning lamp, service compartment has internal lighting; voltage supply can be taken directly from the track or from an independent battery system; has work bench and tool details. This car was to be built on the basic 4060 flatcar chassis in black; length 415 mm. This item will not be produced (G. Nicholson comment), due to cost (J. Hylva comment).   **NA**

CABLE CARS

The Rigi cable cars came in two basic versions both with a sliding side door; all-around glazing, three benches, foldable escape ladder and trap door in floor. Early cars (1978-1979) are of metal construction with rather sharp corners giving them a very boxy shape and are painted red and white with black LGB letters. The more recent versions (1980-1986) are of molded red plastic with white-painted detail. The body corners and edges are more rounded. The single units (i.e. 900 and 900E) may be discontinued for 1986. The 9000S was first offered in 1983 and is still available though it has a limited production.

900 has a single gondola and manual hand crank.   **CP**

900E is the same as 900 with a battery-operated drive unit in plastic box.   **CP**

9000 is the same as 900 with two gondolas and four figures.   **CP**

9000E is the same as 9000 with a battery-operated drive unit with cardboard building to cover drive unit; also has tickets, ticket punch and four figures.   **CP**

9000S is similar to 9000E with green-painted wooden-covered electric (220v) drive unit but lacks figures and other accessories.   **150**

The metal gondola sets are valued at approximately twice the current retail value of their plastic gondola counterparts.

Chapter XI

Publications, Accessories, Track, Catalogues, and other Literature

PUBLICATIONS

Lehmann publications are high quality in material and design, their catalogues (except for the early "menus") being heavy, glossy paper, with well laid out photographs and blocks of text. As the collector market has become more self conscious, interest is growing in this somewhat neglected aspect of the line.

0010: 1971 to date, **Despesche** magazine, a publication by the Lehmann Company about new items, articles on large scale trains, modeling and kit bashing; originally published four times a year (J. Roth comment), then twice a year, now published three times a year, in German language; 21 x 30 cm; enameled paper; pages vary from issue to issue. About $12.00 for annual subscription, although price varies with currency fluctuations.

0010M: 1971-?, miniature **Despesche** magazine; cover is subscription form. Four pages. **10**

0011: 1986 catalogue supplement. **CP**

0011N: 1985-86, a catalogue supplement which lists new LGB items. Comes in both English and German language.
(A) 1985, 11-page supplement with 20150 train set on cover. **NRS**
(B) 1986, unnumbered; the list of discontinued items in the 1986 full catalogue includes the number 0011N. **NRS**

0012: 1974-78, operating instruction manual. 36-page, seven-color booklet in several languages providing basic information on LGB. Some black and white photos, many diagrams, some track plans. Three-page listing of narrow gauge Railroads in Europe. One page listing of model railroad and fan clubs in Germany. Rear cover says "FM5-027-1977." Front cover shows price of booklet in 22 countries. One dated 7/2/76 and one dated 5/2/77. J. Hylva Collection. **NRS**

0012: 1986, counter book with full catalogue line. **CP**

0013: 1978, large glossy photograph poster depicting steeple-cab locomotive with coaches on outdoor layout. **20**

0014: 1978, track planning manual. **NRS**

0015: 1977-86, 135 mm diameter, round sticker for autos (in German). **CP**

0015E: 1983-86, same as 0015, but in English. **CP**

0016: 1983-86, illuminated counter or window sign; shows locomotive and three cars; 220V; length one meter. **CP**

0018: 1985, LGB plastic bag, red, white and green, with LGB logo, "LEHMANN-GROSS-BAHN" and "The Big Train" at top; will hold train set box; 60 x 72 cm. **CP**

0018: 1986, improved carrying bag for train set. **CP**

0019: 1979-85, metal and baked enamel LGB lapel pin. **5**
(A) 1979-80, red with crude "LGB" logo in black; wheels in black and white. **12**
(B) 1980-85, red, yellow and black with well formed "LGB" logo in yellow; 40 x 27 mm. **9**

0020: 1979-86, LGB 62 x 44 cm. color poster.
(A) 1979-82, shows roundhouse scene. **20**
(B) 1983-84, shows 1981 Anniversary train with all anniversary cars. **12**
(C) 1985-86, shows 2096S locomotive opened up to expose electronics. **CP**

0021: 1979-82, parts sheet in German, black-colored cover. **NRS**

0021EPL: 1981-86, EPL directions and use guide; in German, with "foreign" language translations, 24 pages; size 21 x 30 cm. **CP**

0023: 1979-86, manual for operating battery-powered LGB trains. **3**

0024: 1979-86, manual for operating electric LGB trains, in German with "foreign" language translations; two versions; 38 pages, size 15 x 21 cm.
(A) 1979-84, small version, approximately 15 x 20 cm. **3**
(B) 1985-86, larger version, 21 x 30 cm. **CP**

0025: 1979-80, track planning book; softcover, in German. **NRS**

0026: 1980-85, track planning book; hardcover, in German; format 21 x 30 cm, 260 photographs; two tables, 152 pages, 340 illustrations. **16**

0026N: 1985-86, LGB track planning and information book; has 192 pages with 700 photos, plans and layout diagrams; available in German or English. **CP**

0027: 1981-85, **Lehmann Toys - The History of E. P. Lehmann - 1881-1981**; 220 pages; in German. **45**

0027E: 1983-85, same as 0027, in English. **45**

ACCESSORIES

0090: 1971-86, reversing unit for display.
(A) 1971-79, early unit, length 240 cm. **200**
(B) 1980-86, late model, length 120 cm. **CP**

130: Battery powered train direction controller. **CP**

925: 1976, plastic bobsled with two helmeted figures; verification of production requested. **CP**

*NOTE: When all locomotive wheels were changed from "solid" wheels to plastic centers, the crank pin was changed from a machine screw to a self-tapping sheet metal type screw. Thus new wheels cannot be used for replacements for engines with solid wheels unless the new crank pin screws are ordered from the LGB factory; V. Winn comment.

2010/1: Four-piece set of red solid locomotive drive wheels, non-skid tire. **CP**

2010/2: One set of coupling with metal spring and coupling bracket for all twin-axle locomotives. **CP**

2010/3: Standard smokestack. **CP**

2010/4: 10 spare non-skid tires. **CP**

2010/5: Chassis for 2010, 2020 and 2040 locomotives. Will not fit early versions without pickup skates; B. Roth comment. **CP**

2010/7: One set of standard locomotive couplings with plastic spring and coupling bracket. **CP**

2010/27: 10 locomotive buffers, new version with rounded corners and white outlining. **CP**

2015/1: Four-piece set of red-spoked locomotive drive wheels with non-skid tire. **CP**

2015/3: Smokestack with spark arrester. **CP**

2015/5: Chassis for 2015 locomotive. **CP**

2015/6: Two-axle black tender with gear box. **CP**

2017/1: Four-piece set of black-spoked locomotive drive wheels with non-skid tire. **CP**

2017/5: Chassis for 2015 locomotive. **CP**

2017/6: Two-axle green tender with gear box. **CP**

2018/1: Locomotive driving wheels, 46 mm diameter, for 2018. **CP**

2018/4: Traction tires, 46 mm. **CP**

2018/5: Pilot truck for 2018. **CP**

2030/1: Four-piece set of black solid locomotive drive wheels with non-skid tire. **CP**

2030/3: Red pantograph for 2030 locomotive, 2035 trolley or early 2040 crocodile. **CP**

2030/5: Motor block without frame for newer 2030 and 2033 electric locomotives and 2035 and 2036 trams. Older 2030 series locomotives have wires soldered directly to motor housing, and are incompatible with current part; B. Roth comment. **CP**

2035/1: Four-piece set of black solid locomotive drive wheels with non-skid tire. **CP**

2036/3: Electric current collector bow for 2036 trolley. **CP**

2040/1: Four-piece set of black-spoked locomotive drive wheels with non-skid tire. **CP**

2040/2: One set of coupling with plastic spring and pin. **CP**

2040/3: Silver pantograph for 2040 and 2045 electric locomotives. **CP**

2040/5: Set of motor bogies. **CP**

2040/7: One set of standard locomotive couplings with plastic spring and coupling brackets for all rolling stock. Will not fit early locomotives with small coupler loops; B. Roth comment. **CP**

2040/8: Set of 17 insulators, large and small, for 2040 Crocodile. **CP**

2040/9: Eight pieces of plastic springs for universal coupling. **CP**

2040/11: A new lighting module for 2040 crocodile locomotive, can be installed in older versions. **CP**

2051/5: One set of motor bogies for 2051 and 2051S. **CP**

2060/5: Motor block without frame for 2050, 2060, 2060H, 2017 tender. **CP**

2065/1: Four-piece set of black solid locomotive drive wheels without non-skid tire. Will not fit early locomotives without pickup skates; B. Roth comment. **CP**

2065/2: Two steering axle gears. **CP**

2070/0-N: Locomotive truck with lead for 2071D and 2073D; trailing. **CP**

2070/1: Six-piece set of red-spoked locomotive drive wheels with non-skid tire. **CP**

2070/2: One set of coupling with metal spring and coupling bracket for 2071D and 2073D. Will not fit early 2070-2073s unless trailing trucks are replaced; B. Roth comment. **CP**

2070/3: Smokestack with spark arrester. **CP**

2070/5: Chassis, complete with linkage, for 2071D and 2073D. **CP**

2070/7: One set of standard locomotive couplings with plastic spring and coupling bracket for 2071D and 2073D. Will not fit early 2070-2073s unless trailing truck is replaced; B. Roth comment. **CP**

2072/3: Standard smokestack. **CP**

2075/5: Chassis, complete with linkage, for 2075. **CP**

2080/0-V: Locomotive truck for 2080D and 2080S; leading. **CP**

2080/0-N: Locomotive truck with lead for locomotives 2080D and 2080S; trailing. **CP**

2080/1: Six-piece set of red-spoked locomotive drive wheels with non-skid tire. **CP**

2080/2: One set of coupling with metal spring and coupling bracket for 2080D and 2080S. **CP**

2080/3: Smokestack insert for early 2080D or 2080S. **15**

2080/5: Chassis, complete with linkage, for 2080D. **CP**

2085/1: Six-piece set of red-spoked locomotive drive wheels with non-skid tire. **CP**

2085/3: Smokestack insert; 5 volt for 2018D, 2076D, 2080D, 2080S and 2085D. **CP**

2085/5: One set of Mallet motor bogies, with linkage for 2085D. **CP**

2090/1: Four-piece set of red-spoked locomotive drive wheels, with non-skid tire. **CP**

2090/5: Motor block, without frame, with coupling rods, for 2090 and 2090N. **CP**

2090/5: One set of motor bogies, with coupling rods and hall-type crank, for 2095. **CP**

2100: Replacement motor for grinders, one spur gear on motor; last catalogued in 1974-75. **NRS**

2110: Four current pickup carbon brushes. **CP**

2200: Universal DC motor with ball bearings for most railcars. **CP**

2200/6: Gear set for all two and three-axle motor blocks, except 2001 track car. **CP**

2204: DC motor for 2018D and 2045 locomotives. **CP**

2206: DC motor for 2065 railcar and 2066 Wismar bus. **CP**

2210: Two sliding contacts for all locomotives that came with such contacts or pickup skates except 2040. **CP**

2214: Two sliding contacts for 2040 only. **CP**

2218: Two sliding contacts for 2018 D and 2045 locomotives. **CP**

2300: Replacement motor with ball bearings for 2001 track car. May have been a change in motors over the years and current motor will not fit earlier models; V. Winn comment. **CP**

3000/1: Two wheel sets with spoked wheels. **CP**

3000/2: Two wheel bearings for all twin-axle passenger coaches and goods wagons. **CP**

3000/3: Two bogies for 3061, 3062, 3063 and 3064 coaches. **CP**

3000/9: Metalized door handle set. **CP**

3019/1: Two metal wheel sets. **CP**

3019/1: Two sets electrical contacts for additional coach lighting.

3030: 1973-86, interior coach lighting; earliest bulbs were 4-6 volt, for use with batteries, then 12-14 volt, now 18 volt. Change to 12 volt may have come with 3019N lighted baggage car, then later to 18 volts; V. Winn comment. Change to 12 volt came before 3019N; B. Roth comment. **CP**

3031: 1983-86, taillighting. May have been made with 6 volt bulbs; V. Winn comment, confirmed by B. Roth. **CP**

3070/2: Two bogies for 3070 and 3071 coaches. **CP**

3080/2: Two bogies for 3080 and 3081 coaches. **CP**

4000/1: Two wheel sets with disc wheels. **CP**

4000/2: Two bogies for all four-axle goods wagons. **CP**

5000: 1983-85, 220v, variable transformer; 30 volt amps. **15**

5000/110: Same as 5000 for 110v service. **15**

5001: 1971-73, 110v, 1 amp. transformer. **NRS**

5001: 1976-86, LGB smoke and cleaning fluid in 1/4 L container with fill nozzle. **CP**

5001/9: 1986, lubrication and cleaning needle pen, for reaching small holes or tight spots in need of oil. **CP**

5002: 1971-73, 220v, 1 amp. transformer. **NRS**

5002: 1983-85, Five-piece tool set consisting of two screwdrivers, two nut drivers and a wire stripper. **CP**

5003: 1971-82, 220v, 1 amp. variable transformer. **NRS**

5003/110: 1971-82, same as 5003 in 110v. **NRS**

5003/110: 1986, new United States version in gray plastic; sold separately and with 1985-86 sets. **CP**

5004: 1969-86, track cleaning block with 20 grade sandpaper. **5**

5005: 1971-86, automatic rail cleaning unit for attachment to 300 mm cars. Improved in 1986 by replacing sandpaper pieces with pieces of abrasive sponge. **CP**

5006: 1981-86, 220v, 2 amp. transformer for use with 5007 speed controller. **NRS**

5006/110v: 1981-86, 110v, same as 5006. Catalogued but not produced in 110 volt version; G. Nicholson comment. **NRS**

5007: 1984-86, electronic speed controller with cruise-control, brake, accelerator, etc.; can be used on AC or DC transformers. **65**

5008: 1971-80, high performance 220v, 2 amp. transformer for use with 5012 speed controller. **NRS**

5009: 1971, electronic cockpit control with transformer, 220v, 2 amp. **NRS**

5009: 1986, power booster for power packs; will double amperage. **CP**

5010: 1969-72, speed controller with brown protective housing, black roof. **NRS**

5012: 1971-82, outdoor speed controller with similar housing as 5010 but in green; carries up to 1.5 amps. **45**

5012N: 1983-86, speed controller in signal box. **CP**

5013: 1983-86, double-strand roll of wire, orange and white; length 20 m; twin-core lead. **CP**

5013/1: 1983-86, wire terminal plugs for crimping on wire ends; pack of 50. **CP**

5014: 1983-86, double-strand roll of wire, black and white; length 20 cm; twin core lead. **CP**

5015: 1979-86, cable to link transformer to speed controller; length 500 cm; connecting and extension cable with terminals. **CP**

5015/1: 1979-86, electrical eyelet connectors for use on threaded poles; pack of 10. **CP**

5016: 1969-86, cable with clamp lugs linking speed controller and transformer to track; early versions have small all metal track clamps, while later versions have larger plastic track clamps with metal lining and bolt. Although the newer clamp is catalogued separately as item 1600 as early as 1979-80, catalogue pictures of 5016 continue to show the older metal lugs until 1985. Connecting lead, length 150 cm. **CP**
(A) 1969-79?-84?, with older all metal lugs. **NRS**
(B) 1979?-1984?-86?, with newer plastic mounted clamps and screws. **CP**

5016/1: 1979-86, two track terminals for clamping electrical feed wires to track, without wires; never available in the small all metal version, these have large plastic bodies with metal lining and screws. **CP**

5016/5000: 1981-86, cable wire suppressor, heavy duty; length 150 cm. **CP**

5016/5000N: 1977-78, early version of 5016/5000; length 150 cm. **NRS**

5016/5003: 1977-82, high performance cable with suppressor; length 150 cm; heavy-duty connecting cable. **CP**

5016/5012: 1977-85, high performance cable with suppressor; length 150 cm; heavy-duty connecting cable. **CP**

5017: 1971-85, cable linking 5075 switch box to remote switch track. **CP**

5018: 1971-86, similar to 5017 with double-strand wire; control box cable, length 200 cm. **CP**

5019: 1973-85, single-strand cable linking 5080 control box to transformer; control box cable 200 cm. **CP**

5020: 1973-85, similar to 5019, but links control box to track. **CP**

5021: 1973-86, single-strand cable linking track to track; jumper lead, length 300 cm. **CP**

5022: 1979-86, roll of single-strand gray wire; single core lead; length 40 m. **CP**

5023: 1981-86, roll of double-strand wire, blue and red; twin core lead; length 20 m. **CP**

5024: 1981-85, roll of triple-strand wire, green, white and yellow; three core lead; length 20 m. **CP**

5025: 1974-86, wheel stop blocks for rails; pack of 12. **CP**

5026: 1974-86, yellow plastic rail joiners for isolation, pack of four; rail isolating clips. **CP**

5026: 1986, far west travelers; includes child, lady, frontier farmer, gentleman with top hat. **CP**

5027: 1985-86, circus animals and trainer; includes seven standing figures: chimpanzee, lion, elephant, camel, rhinocerous and polar bear and a trainer wearing a red turban and blue vest. **CP**

5029: 1973-82, electromagnetic semaphore signal with lighting. **30**

5029: 1986, baggage and crates. **CP**

5030: 1971-86, same as 5029 but manual control. Early issues snapped to track but later issues had less fragile movable snap lock; B. Roth comment. **CP**

5030/1: 1971-86, replacement arm for Prussian semaphore. **CP**

5031: 1983-86, set of 27 different subsidiary signals. **NRS**

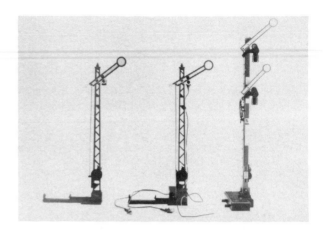

The two older signals, 5030 manual at left and 5029, lighted with electric throw, in center; both have the original snap-on base for attaching to track rather than the later slide-on piece, and both are in the "proceed" position. At right is signal 5094, with wires concealed in mast; its lights show green over yellow in the "proceed" position which, like the two arms, means proceed slowly. When the arms move to "stop" they rotate in opposite directions, so that one aligns invisibly with the mast and the other drops to horizontal. The "stop" signal thus is the same as for a one-arm signal, rather than confusingly different; both lights then show red.

5031/1: 1973-86, replacement arm for Bavarian semaphore. **CP**

5032: 1973-86, warning signs; set of 16. **CP**

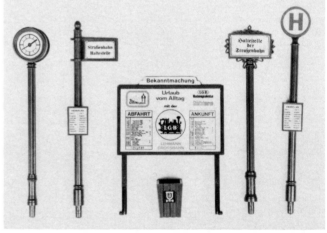

The four signs of tram stop set 5033 may represent different historical periods, and presumably should not be mounted on the same platform.

5033: 1977-78, two tram stop posts. **NRS**

5033: 1983-86, tram stop set; eight pieces. **CP**

5034: 1979-86, street level station platform; 12 pieces — eight broad, four narrow. **CP**

5035: 1973-81, standard telephone pole. **NRS**

5035: 1981-86, telephone pole with no supports, used on straight track; telephone poles are not necessarily designed to run along side of track. **NRS**

5036: 1973-86, telephone pole with single side support; used on curves. **CP**

5038: 1979-86, advertising column; outdoor advertising pillar with various period and modern posters. **CP**

5040: 1969-73, four station figures, Set I: station master with signal disc, conductor, man and woman passengers.
(A) 1969-73, man is wearing hat and woman is carrying umbrella. **NRS**
(B) 1974-86, man not wearing hat and woman is carrying suitcases. **CP**

Three sets of people are hand-painted in the Nuremberg area as a cottage industry. From left to right: Top: 5040, station figures, including two passengers and two trainmen, one with ticket bag and the other with train signal on a movable arm, and 5042, seated passengers. Middle: 5043, more station figures, including a porter, a paper vender, a track worker and an oiler and 5044, more station figures, including a passenger with poodle, a nurse, a porter with cart of bags and a track worker. Bottom: 5045, more station figures, including a waiter, a sandwich vendor, a trainman with lantern and an engineer with wrench; 5047, four seated travelers, including hobo and a black couple. G. Ryall Collection

5041: 1969-85, six figures in traditional dress of the Black Forest. **CP**

5042: 1969-86, four seated figures in business and traditional dress.
(A) 1969-73, two men in Alpine attire, identical except one with black vest, gray hat and one with green vest and hat, and two women, identical except one with red dress and one with blue dress. **NRS**
(B) 1974-86, two different couples, one woman in blue dress and one man in Alpine attire with black vest, gray hat; new couple added as introduced as 2035/3500 tram passengers. **CP**

5043: 1971-86, four-figure station personnel set: engine oiler, porter, newspaper man and track workman. Figures may be painted different colors; C. Colwell comment. **CP**

5044: 1973-86, four station figures, Set II: porter with hand-cart, Red Cross worker, waving girl with dog and track worker with shovel. **CP**

5045: 1971-74, battery-operated signal baton as used by station master. **NRS**

5045: 1977-86, four station figures, Set III: engine fitter with wrench, conductor with lamp, waiter and Bratwurst vendor. **CP**

5046: 1979-86, six figure tourist group: hikers with backpacks, man with camera, two skiiers. **CP**

5047: 1980-86, four seated figures, Set I: black couple, teenager, tramp. **CP**

5048: 1980-86, four standing passengers; includes man and woman greeting each other, motorcyclist with helmet, woman with moped cycle. **CP**

5049: 1985, U.S. figures of the 19th century; includes six standing figures: well-dressed traveling couple, sheriff, hobo, railroad conductor and telegraph operator. **CP**

5050: 1969-86, station lamp; height 210 mm. **CP**

5050/1: 1975-86, universal screw-in replacement bulbs; set of 25; yellow lens. **CP**

5050/2: 1983-86, two bulb sockets and wire lead. **CP**

5051/1: 1981-86, white plug-in micro bulbs for locomotives and cars; set of 10. **CP**

5051/2: 1981-86, same as 5051/1, but in red. **CP**

5052: 1983-86, illuminated warning light for terminal track buffers. **CP**

5055: 1984-86, single-arm station lamp with shade and bulb; height 335 mm. **CP**

5056: 1984-86, double-arm station lamp with shades and bulbs; height 335 mm. **CP**

5060: 1969-86, railway trestle bridge; length 450 mm. **CP**

5061: 1986, 1200 trestle bridge (outside height 300 mm, inside height 224 mm); comes with supports to provide track with gradual incline. **CP**

Railroad crossing 5065 includes road grading to fit over the track, which sits on spring levers that lower the gates when depressed by the weight of a passing train. G. Ryall Collection

5065: 1973-85, level crossing barrier with mechanical arms; length 250 mm; width 310 mm. **CP**

5070: 1969-82, multi-pole wiring terminal plate; distributor strip.
(A) 1969-76, gray plate with two poles. **NRS**
(B) 1977-80, yellow plate with three poles. **NRS**
(C) 1981-82, gray plate with three poles. **3**

5071: 1979-85, trackside cable holders; pack of five. **CP**

5072: 1983-85, two pole wiring terminal block; distribution box. **CP**

5073: 1983-85, twelve pole wiring terminal block; connecting block. **CP**

5075: 1971-82, switch control box for operating track switches and other electromagnetic mechanisms. **CP**

5075N: 1983-85, same as 5075, for use with EPL mechanisms. **CP**

5075/1: 1973-85, 5075 or 5075N decal sheet of control box signs. **CP**

5080: 1981-82, control box with protective lid for lights and other connect/disconnect mechanisms. **CP**

5080N: 1983-85, same as 5080, for use with EPL mechanisms. **CP**

5080/1: 1971-85, 5080 or 5080N decal sheet of control box signs. **CP**

Pictured from left to right: Distant Signal; the same distant signal, with disk up; three "signal ahead" boards that come with each signal and 5093 Distant Signal with rotating arrow. G. Ryall Collection

5090: 1981-85, electromagnetic mechanism for actuating semaphore signals. **CP**

5091: 1981-85, distant warning signal with movable signal disc; light changes from yellow to green; height 230 mm. **CP**

5092: 1981-85, home stop signal with single arm and light change; height 350 mm. **CP**

5093: 1981-85, two form distant warning signal with fixed disc, movable arm and light change; height 230 mm. **CP**

5094: 1983-85, two form home stop signal with two arms and double lights, height 350 mm. **CP**

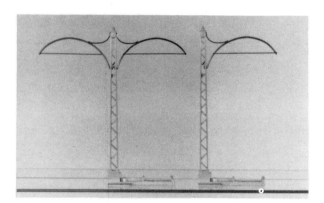

Catenary support 6000 can be fitted with single or double arms to hold overhead wires which can function as electric feeds through engine pantographs, making independent control of two trains possible; one rail of track is common to both control circuits. Models of electric engines have a switch for selection of overhead, rather than track, power.

6000: 1971-85, catenary mast; early masts only snapped to track (the catch often broke); later masts have a movable snap lock. **CP**

6000/2: 1971-85, catenary mast support arm; mast bracket arm. **CP**

6001: 1971-85, catenary mast connection; feeder mast, similar to 6000. **CP**

6009: 1979-85, catenary wires to change direction of current collector bow; pack of two. **CP**

6010: 1971-85, catenary wire for track 1000; length 300 mm. **CP**

6011: 1971-85, catenary wire for track 1100; length 315 mm. **CP**

6015: 1979-85, catenary wire for track 1500; length 400 mm. **CP**

6016: 1979-85, catenary wire for track 1600; length 470 mm. **CP**

6060: 1979-85, catenary wire for track 1060; length 600 mm. **CP**

6100: 1981-85, aluminum catenary mast; maximum height 365 mm. **CP**

6100/2: 1981-85, contact-wire support arms. **CP**

6100/4: 1981-85, metal connectors for catenary (pack of 12); these are sold separately as well as in boxed sets. **CP**

6100/5: 1981-85, plastic connectors for catenary (pack of 12); these are sold separately as well as in boxed sets. **CP**

6101: 1981-85, contact wire support arm for catenary; cable length 1 m each. **CP**

6102: 1981-85, gantry supports for catenary, pack of three. **CP**

6160: 1981-85, twelve-piece contact wire kit with 600 mm wire for catenary. **CP**

6190: 1981-85, twelve-piece contact wire kit with 900 mm wire for catenary. **CP**

TRACK

In the early 1970s Lehmann manufactured track with aluminum as well as brass rail. The catalogue numbers of these track sections were basically the same; but the brass track originally had the letter "W" for weather proof added to its number, i.e. early brass 300 mm track sections had the catalogue number "1000w". Lehmann dropped the "W"

designation when they ceased production of the aluminum track about 1977-1978; to avoid confusion, the "W" designation has not been used in this book.

100: Plastic straight track. **CP**

110: Plastic curved track. **CP**

120: Plastic Y-switch track. **CP**

1000: 1971-86, straight track section; length 300 mm.
(A) 1971-78, aluminum rails. **3**
(B) 1969-85, brass rails. **CP**

1000K(1000KW): 1971-82, reverse loop kit in two sections for polarity reversal; rectifying diodes concealed under simulated grade crossing; length 2 x 300 mm.
(A) No green dot on diode section. **NRS**
(B) Has green dot on diode section. **NRS**

1000/T: 1969-82, isolation track interrupts current flow to both rails of track; length 300 mm. **NRS**

1000/U: 1971-82, isolation track interrupts current flow to both rails of track; length 300 mm. **NRS**

1000/1: 1978-86, pack of 10 brass rail joiners. **CP**

1000/2: 1978-85, assortment of 100 self-tapping screws in four sizes and assorted knurled nuts. **CP**

1000/3: 1981-86, flexible sleeper bed section, pack of five; can be used as replacement or for 1.5 m track sections. **CP**

1000/5: 1981-86, 1.5 m brass rail sections. **CP**

1001: 1974-79, track planning template. **NRS**

1001N: 1980-84, track planning template which includes 1400 turntable. **CP**

1002: 1986, wheel guide for placing locomotives or rolling stock on track; made of orange plastic. **CP**

1004: 1979-86, brass track section; length 41 mm. **CP**

1005: 1979-86, brass track section; length 52 mm. **CP**

1006: 1986, 150 mm plastic adaptor track for joining regular brass track sections with the plastic track sections of the battery-operated trains. **CP**

1007: 1984-86, brass track section; length 75 mm. **CP**

1008: 1971-86, brass track section; length 82 mm. **CP**

1009: 1979-86, expandable brass track section; variable length 88-120 mm. **CP**

1015: 1983-86, brass track section; length 150 mm. **CP**

1015K: 1983-86, reverse loop kit in two sections designed for use with EPL system; length 2 x 150 mm. **CP**

Illuminated track-end bumper 1031, at left, simulates a sturdy construction of timbers filled with gravel. To its right, electrically operated uncoupler 1056, with indicator light so the operator may read the ramp position from a distance. At far right is light 5050, after an old-fashioned prototype; and in front, a section of platform 5034, which fits between and beside straight tracks for pedestrian crossing. G. Ryall Collection

1015T: 1983-86, isolation track, both rails; length 150 mm.   **CP**

1015U: 1983-86, isolation track, one rail; length 150 mm.   **CP**

1021: 1986, 300 mm rack section for use with 2046 rack locomotive.   **CP**

1022: 1986, rack section lock pieces for securing 1021 to track.   **CP**

1030: 1969-85, standard terminal track buffer (not illuminated).   **4**

1031: 1981-86, same as 1030, but with illuminated warning light; buffer stop with "stop" (dead-end) signal.   **CP**

1050: 1969-82, brass manual uncoupling track; length 300 mm.   **16**

1052: 1971-86, standard permanent uncoupler.
(A) 1971-80, larger size, red-colored parts; coil spring, button action.   **NRS**
(B) 1981-86, slightly slimmer, black-colored parts; leaf spring, lever action.   **CP**

1055: 1974-83, remote electromagnetic uncoupler; length 300 mm.   **CP**

1056: 1984-86, electromagnetic uncoupler similar to 1055 but suited for use with EPL equipment.
(A) 1984-85, length 300 mm.   **CP**
(B) 1985-86, length 150 mm.   **CP**

1060: 600 mm; brass track section.   **CP**

1102, 1100 and 1500 Track Sections. G. Ryall Collection

1100: 1971-86, 120 cm diameter curved 30 degree track section.
(A) 1971-78, aluminum rails.   **20**
(B) 1969-85, brass rails.   **CP**

1102: 1984-86, half curved brass track.   **CP**

1104: 1981-86, short curved 7.5 degree brass make-up track section.   **CP**

1150: 1969-86, track clips for securing track on temporary layouts; set of 28.   **CP**

1200: 1969-82, right-hand manual switch track; same radius as 1100 curved track.
(A) 1969-75, early housing with pivoting throw arm; attached directly to track; switch machine not removable.   **10**
(B) 1976-82, later housing with sliding actuating arm.   **20**

1200N
(A) 1983-85, same as 1200, but with latest actuating box, which is smaller than those of previous units and square-shaped; length 300 mm.   **CP**
(B) 1985-86, same as (A) but with unjointed point rails, continuous from plastic frog to point blade, pivoted at the frog itself, rather than halfway from frog to blade as (A) is.   **CP**

1201: 1983-86, EPL points drive mechanism.   **CP**

1203: 1983-86, additional switch for EPL drive mechanism; used in conjunction with 1201.   **CP**

1204: 1983-86, rotatable switch lantern; for use with 1201.   **CP**

1205: 1971-82, right-hand, remote switch track with 1206 electromagnetic switching mechanism; same radius as 1100.   **26**

1205N
(A) 1983-85, same as 1205, but with 1201 EPL switch drive mechanism; length 300 mm.   **CP**

Arranged chronologically from left to right, four minimum radius switches: 1200(A), its large pivoting switch mechanism permanently housed beneath an unlighted lantern (visible from the top as a square) that serves as a throw handle; the wires, visible where the point rails pivot, were added to improve electrical contact. 1200(B), the same switch with a much improved sliding actuating arm, in a removable box that can be attached at either side. 1210N (1983-1985), with a prototypical cover plate over the point throw bar, and shiny added electrical contacts at the point ends; the box houses the 1201 electrical points drive mechanism. The newest switch, at right, is 1200N (1985-1986), with continuous, unbroken rails from frog to point; the moving point rails pivot at the plastic frog, rather than halfway between, thereby eliminating one electrical joint; and a small manual throw.

(B) 1985-86, same as (A), but with unjointed point rails, continuous from plastic frog to point blade, pivoted at the frog itself, rather than halfway from frog to blade as (A) is.

1206: 1974-82, early electromagnetic switch actuator.   **8**

1207: 1974-82, rotatable switch lantern for use with 1206; non-illuminated.   **3**

1208: 1981-82, electric drive mechanism for actuating switches. This unit was rarely used and may have only been used on the 1235 three-way switch.   **NRS**

1209: 1982-85, electric drive motor for 1225 slip switch. Early 1209s do not have replaceable drive motor; B. Roth comment.   **CP**

1210: 1969-82, left-hand manual switch track; same radius as 1100 curved track; similar to 1200(A).
(A) 1969-75, early housing with pivoting throw arm.   **NRS**
(B) 1976-82, later housing with sliding actuating arm.   **20**

1210N
(A) 1983-85, same as 1210, but with latest actuating box which is smaller than those of previous units and square-shaped; length 300 mm.   **CP**
(B) 1985-86, same as (A) but with unjointed point rails, continuous from plastic frog to point blade, pivoted at the frog itself, rather than halfway from frog to blade as (A) is.   **CP**

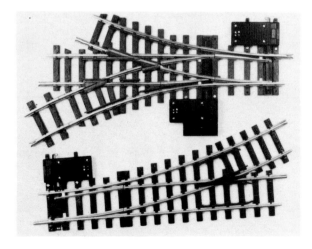

1235 Three-way Turnout and 1615 Left-hand Remote Switch Track.

1211: 1981-82, rotatable illuminated switch lantern for use with 1206. **6**

1215: 1971-82, left-hand, remote switch track with 1206 electromagnetic switching mechanism. **26**

1215N
(A)1983-85, same as 1215, but with 1201 EPL drive mechanism; length 300 mm. **CP**
(B)1985-86, same as (A), but with unjointed point rails, continuous from plastic frog to point blade, pivoted at the frog itself, rather than halfway from frog to blade as (A) is. **CP**

1225: 1979-85, 22.5 degree double-slip switch driven by electric motor mechanism 1209; length 2 x 375 mm. **CP**

1226: 1985-86, double-slip switch with two electromagnetic operating mechanisms; for use with 22.5 degree curves (1600 curved track); total length 375 mm. **CP**

1235: 1981-82, three-way turnout driven by two separate drive mechanisms; has same radius as 1600 curved track.
(A) 1981-?, has 1208 drive mechanisms. **NRS**
(B) 1980-82, has 1206 drive mechanisms. **CP**

1235N: 1983-85, same as 1235, but with 1201 EPL drive mechanisms. **CP**

1236: 1985-86, three-way switch with two electromagnetic operating mechanisms for use with 30 degree curved track (1100 curved track); total length 375 mm. **CP**

1300: 1971-86, 30 degree brass crossing track; length 300 and 341 mm.
  CP

1225 Double Slip Switch and 1320 Crossing. G. Ryall Collection

1320: 1982-86, 22.5 degree brass crossing track; length 2 x 375 mm. **CP**

1400: 1979-86, manual turntable with 65 cm diameter; handmade, not weather proof. **CP**

1500: 1971-86, 155 cm diameter curved 30 degree brass track. **CP**

1600: 1975-83, 235 cm diameter curved 22.5 degree brass track. **CP**

1605: 1975-85, right-hand, remote switch track with the same radius as the 1600 curved track; 1206 actuating mechanism. **CP**

1605N: 1983-86, same as 1605, but with 1201 EPL drive mechanism. **CP**

1615: 1975-82, left-hand version of the 1605. **CP**

1615N: 1983-86, left-hand version of 1605N; length 440 mm. **CP**

1700: 1983-85, track contact for automatic switching operations; actuated by 1701 switching magnet. The first version of this unit is depicted in the 1981-82 catalogue. It is an "H"-shaped mechanism with a brass shoe and a single-wire version which was never produced. The unit which finally saw production is shown in the 1983-84 catalogue and is more elongated with two small boxes — one for the switch mechanism and one for the connecting wires. **CP**

1701: 1983-86, switching magnet for attaching on the bottom of the locomotives to automatically actuate 1700 contact switch. **CP**

1900: 1981-85, toporama layout (242 x 395 cm). **CP**

2060/3: 1978-86, contact strip for triggering horn on 2051S, 2060H and 2096S locomotives and whistle bell on 2080S; length 300 mm. **CP**
2060H3: 1975-78, early number for 2060/3 contact strip. **CP**

20901: 1977-85, buffers track pack set; includes six 1000s, one 1100, one 1200 or 1200N, one 1030. **CP**

20902: 1979-85, station track pack set; includes nine 1000s, two 1100s, one 1200 or 1200N, one 1210 or 1210N. **CP**

CATALOGUES & LITERATURE

Catalogues were generally published every two years; however, several catalogue-like brochures were printed at different intervals.

1968: Single sheet flyer, first literature describing product: "Premiere 10-16 Februar 1968 auf der Internationalen Spielwarenmesse in Nurnberg! Stand 2001" German text, black and white with some green lettering and a green track plan; photos show a 2020-type steam locomotive with flaring stack and pale cab, but number "4" on cab as if 2040; 3010 and 3000 (no number listed); also the Richter children playing with those items, with what looks like a 3011, and with some track; a silhouette drawing on the reverse includes a 4020 or 4021. Five of the nine photographs and five of the seven paragraphs, slightly edited, appear as page three of 1968-69 catalogue. C. Colwell Collection. **NRS**

Circa 1968-69: Catalogue, eight pages, no date but has very few items in it; along with prices in German. Cover depicts the 2010 locomotive and in the right-hand corner mentions shown in "original size". Catalogue is black and white and has patches of orange throughout. Variation: Does not have "original size" in right-hand corner but the words "Lehmann" in big black letters. Also the last three pages are different. The one with "Lehmann" has a replacement motor listed along with spare pickup shoes, among other things; J. Hylva comment. Sold for 25DM (cash $10.00) in Nuremberg and for $45.00 in the United States in 1985. **45**

1969-70 Catalogue.

1969-70: A 13-page color catalogue with the cover depicting an early 2010 locomotive pulling four cars (3000, 3010, 3015 and 3020), also has the "LGB" logo and "Lehmann Gross-Bahn 1969-70" in black on front cover; rear cover depicts a 3000 coach in blue, however this is due to the color separations and is not an unusual variation of this car. English, French or German; 210 x 270 mm. **55**

1970: A 58-page color catalogue, undated (date identified by W. Richter), with a tight overhead scene on the cover of a 2060, 2020, 4040S, 4041, 3010, 3009, 2050 and 4040E on several parallel tracks with a station and freight house between; "Lehmann" in upper right corner, "Die Welt der L.G.B." (green letters, beige logo) in lower right corner. Rear cover is a head-on shot of a 2010 pulling 3011, 3010, 3012 and 3040; beside it, a 2060G pulls a 4040S, a blue 4040A (which does not appear inside; only the gray 4040A is catalogued), and 4040E. 31 interior pages in color. 210 x 150 mm. C. Colwell Collection. **NRS**

1970-71: A black and white single page, folded six ways; date is not shown on cover. Cover shows 2010 pulling two freight cars, 2030 pulling one freight car, 2050 pulling two coaches, two 2060s pulling three freight cars, 2020 pulling two and one-half coaches, all from an overhead view on four sidings. Rear cover depicts different sets, in German; J. Hylva comment.

20

1971: Four-page black and white folder showing new items and price changes for 1969-70 catalogue. Many new pieces listed; locomotives 2030, 2070, etc.; in English; D. Weiler comment. **NRS**

1971-72 Catalogue.

1971-72: A black and white single page, 885 x 420 mm unfolded, with three folds making six sheets; date is not shown; cover shows a 2060Y diesel locomotive, a 2020 steam locomotive, an early 2001 track inspection car and a 2030 steeple-cab electric locomotive; a young boy and girl are in the background. German or English; J. Barton and D. Weiler comment; 210 x 296 mm folded; 2020 on cover has late 1974 detailing, but round roof vent; J. Barton comment. **30**

1972: Orange cover supplement catalogue, lists accessories for LGB trains from companies like Mossmer, Lindberg, Fischer, Herpa, etc; J. Hylva comment. **NRS**

1972-73: Similar to 1971-72 (black and white single page, 885 x 420 mm unfolded, with three folds making six sheets), but with "Auf LGB umsteigen-einsteigen-abfahren!" in green: "Programm 72-73" in green in lower right corner; LGB logo, white on green, upper right corner. Cover shows 2010 pulling into station, with people sitting on bench under a covered platform. Rear cover depicts various sets. 210 x 296 mm folded. J. Hylva and D. Weiler comments. **NRS**

1973-74: Similar to 1972-73 (black and white single page with green highlights, 885 x 420 mm unfolded, with three folds making six sheets), but with date in upper right corner; "The Giant Railway with the Guarantee for Great Fun" in green letters upper left corner; LGB logo, white on green, lower right. Cover shows 3080 pulling 4063 and 4066, and 2095 pulling 4062; 5065 and 5029 also shown. Printed in both English and German. Folded, 210 x 296 mm. **45**

1974: Single sheet in color; "Die Grosse Bahn fur Haus und Garten" on front, with pictures of 4043, 2010, 2030, 3050, 4040E (ET) and 4042; 2030 pulling two 3011s and two 3012s on back; German text; 210 x 297 mm; B. Roth comment. **NRS**

1974: Similar to preceding (single sheet, color, 210 x 297 mm) but with "Die Grosse Bahn Fahrt in der Kleinsten Hutte" on cover; indoor layout on back. **NRS**

1974-75: A color, single-folded page, 260 x 1775 mm unfolded, with seven vertical creases; date is shown in the lower right-hand corner of the front cover; cover depicts anterior aspects of 2070 steam and 2095 diesel locomotives; English or German; 185 x 260 mm folded. **26**

1974-75 Catalogue.

1975: Single sheet, in German, printed in black and white; 2080S and 2015 (prototype model) on front; various cars on back; 210 x 290 mm; B. Roth comment. **NRS**

1975-76: A color catalogue of twelve pages including covers, which folded in half is 185 x 260 mm; unfolded but not opened, 365 x 260 mm; opened, 725 x 260 mm. Cover shows side view of 2080; "Die Grosse Bahn. 75-76" in red with an arrow in place of the hyphen; "Das LGB-Programm" above the date in black; green shield around yellow LGB. English and German; J. Hylva comment. **NRS**

1976: New items sheet; single sheet folded; color and black and white; prototype model of 2035 shown on cover, German only; W. Gallagher comment. **NRS**

1977: Trifold color flyer with, inside, larger than lifesize photo of 2017; on front: "Hobby, Fun and Recreation", "LGB" and collage photos; English 310 x 650 mm; B. Roth comment. **NRS**

1977-78 Catalogue.

1977-78: An 18-page color catalogue with the cover depicting the same roundhouse scene utilized on the early 0020 458 x 610 mm color poster; English or German; 240 x 344 mm unopened. **25**

1978: Black and white supplement, six pages, shows new item for 1978 like 2040, 2036 and 3600, 4040C, etc.; J. Hylva comment. **NRS**

1979-80: First of the big color catalogues. Cover has two horizontal yellow stripes with the "LGB" logo and a round photograph of an 0-4-0T locomotive with the Lehmann plant in the background. 96 numbered pages plus cover pages; 210 x 302 mm.

(A) German version has a semi-glossy black cover. **20**

(B) English version has a semi-glossy red cover. **20**

1980: Black and white supplement, four pages; shows new items for 1980 like 2065, 2051S, 2060H (new horn location), new catenary, etc.; J. Hylva comment. **NRS**

1979-80 Catalogue.

1981-82: The Jubilee catalogue to commemorate "100 Years of Lehmann", very glossy black cover, 128 numbered pages plus cover pages.

(A) German version with "100 JAHRE" lettered in green; inside rear cover depicts scenes with well-known German personalities enjoying LGB. Page 78 shows very early prototypes of the 3080 and 3081 coaches without markings and with unpainted roofs.   **12**

(B) English version with "100 YEARS" lettered in red on upper right of cover; inside rear cover depicts a group of Lehmann factory personnel.   **10**

(C) Same as (B), with standard production models of the 3080 and 3081 coaches depicted on page 78; 5009 and 5010 deleted from page 105.   **10**

1981-82: Unnumbered — condensed catalogue in English. Spiral bound with same cover as Main Jubilee Catalogue "100 Years of Lehmann", but containing only the summary pages: "Advantages of the LGB", "Locomotives at a Glance" and "LGB Track Range". Also included are several pages depicting their toy line and Rigi Cable Cars; W. Gallagher comment.

1983-84: Very glossy, deep maroon-red cover; two stripes and large "LGB" logo, 160 numbered pages plus covers.

1984 Catalogue.

(A) German version has gold stripes on maroon red and "LGB" logo only on the front cover.   **6**

(B) English version has silver stripes on maroon red, "LGB" logo and the words "The Big Train" all in silver on the front cover.   **6**

1984: Brochure, six pages folded twice with 2010 locomotive on color cover. Opens up to three pages wide which shows all the LGB displayed on the floor with admiring people in the background; J. Hylva comment.   **CP**

1984: 100 Years of Lehmann, 16 pages plus color cover with 2010 locomotive on black background, similar to 1981-82 catalogue cover; has plastic binding holding it together. Shows all LGB models inside; sort of a condensed catalogue; J. Hylva comment.   **CP**

1984-85: Same as the 1983-84 version except the stripes are white with a green stripe in the middle and the LGB logo and "The Big Train" in white print.   **CP**

1985: English version with white engine on maroon cover with green stripe; an updated version of 1983-84 catalogue; 160 numbered pages plus cover. German version only; G. Nicholson comment.

1985 Catalogue.

1985: Supplemental Catalogue OO11N; 1985 in red letters on white background with 150 red Jubilee anniversary engine on front cover; eight pages.   **1**

1986-87: Cover has photo of 2045 locomotive, back cover has aerial photograph of Lehmann factory. 112 pages. Produced in English and German. This will be the last of the biannual catalogues; beginning 1987 a new catalogue will be produced each year to keep up with new items; W. Richter comment.

*Different Items

A poster board folded twice with glossy finish depicting all of the 1972-73 catalogue; J. Hylva comment.   **NRS**

"Lots of Fun w/LGB" booklet. 24 pages with 2010 engine on cover. Bottom half of cover is orange, 15 x 21 cm size, early 1970s. Sort of an instruction manual printed in seven languages; J. Hylva comment.   **NRS**

Date not known, four-page, brown matte-type brochure depicting American prototypes. Possibly issued by LGB National Sales Office, Milwaukee, WI; J. Hylva comment.   **NRS**

Index